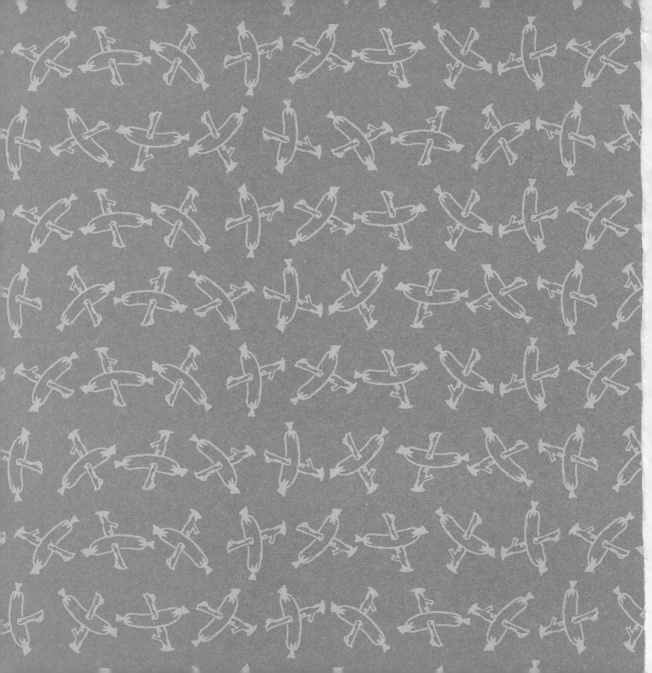

VANESSA BANTE

GIBBS SMITH
TO ENRICH AND INSPIRE HUMANKIND

To fruition and the dream
of forever happiness with you.

20 19 18 17 16   5 4 3 2 1

Text and photographs © 2016 by Vanessa Bante
Except photographs on pages 17, 23, 25 and 27 from
Shutterstock

Published by
Gibbs Smith
P.O. Box 667
Layton, Utah 84041

1.800.835.4993 orders
www.gibbs-smith.com

Designed by Sheryl Dickert
Page production by Sky Hatter

Gibbs Smith books are printed on paper produced from
sustainable PEFC-certified forest/controlled wood source.
Learn more at www.pefc.org.

Printed and bound in Hong Kong

Library of Congress Control Number: 2015949763
ISBN: 978-1-4236-4172-8

Contents

Acknowledgments

I would like to send a special thank-you to my parents for their constant support and for helping me cook all the delicious dishes created around the fire pit in the backyard. I am so appreciative to them both for teaching me at a young age how to cook in a fire pit on our many camping trips and for taking a long drive to Lake Erie that turned out to be a bust. I appreciate them allowing me to use their fire pit for the majority of the photos and for helping me build a fake beach in the backyard.

I want to thank Aunt Monica and Uncle Ron for letting me use their fire pit to take some amazing fire and food shots.

I would like to thank the rest of my family, especially my sister Samantha and cousin Kayla, for all their support and constant positive feedback toward this new venture in my life.

I want to also send a special thanks to Nick Gill for helping me in editing the photos and for teaching me how to take better shots of food. I learned a great deal from his tips and tricks with photography. A very special thank-you to my first editor, Madge Baird, for always being there for me with any questions I needed answered and for supporting the vision of the book from beginning to end. I am very grateful, as I never could have completed this cookbook without her. Thanks also to associate editor Kerry McShane for refining the recipes; I appreciate all of her hard work and dedication to the outcome of the book.

I am grateful to all of the campfire and fire pit manufacturers for providing all their knowledge and products for purchase. May they never stop inventing new tools and methods for cooking with fire. Here's to a fire pit in every backyard!

Introduction

Fire pits have taken the world by storm, with a wide-ranging variety of rustic styles and modern shapes to suit any person's interest. Whether you and your family are cozied up to a backyard fire pit on a starry winter night or camping in the mountains in early spring you can find nearly any form of fire pit to suit your needs.

I highly recommend placing a fire pit permanently in your backyard if you have space. Start by digging a hole; then stack up some blocks purchased at a home store or line it with a metal fire pit ring liner. Cooking over a fire is more than preparing food—it is a great way to entertain friends and family and provide a source of heat on a cold night.

If you don't want to dig a hole for a permanent fire pit, you can purchase an aboveground or patio version. Some of these are transportable.

Practically every flavor-filled recipe here provides a newer way to enjoy the comforting foods we all love. This book highlights several basic techniques of cooking, grilling and baking inside a fire pit, using familiar camping tools and a few others that can be found in and around your home. Everyone in the family can be a part of cooking around a fire pit, so let this book inspire some exciting new cooking fun!

Following is a rundown of fire pit types, advice on fire building, and an overview of useful cooking equipment and tools.

Types of Fire Pits

WOOD-BURNING GRILL OR FIRE PIT GRILL: Specifically designed for fire pit cooking. Most come with a grill grate that fits on the pit or on top of the firewood embers.

PORTABLE FIRE PIT: A number of manufacturers make these, in a variety of styles and materials. The portable pits generally have a large bowl with legs and a mesh lid. Some also include a grill grate that can be placed on top.

FIRE PIT TABLE: There is a wide selection of fire pits build into an outdoor table or having a table-like rim surrounding the pit. Ultimately, this style comes in handy for resting beverages and food while enjoying the fire but also provides a place to rest the fire pit tool handles while the food cooks to perfection.

CAST-IRON FIRE PIT: Cast iron lasts a long time. It is solid, strong, and moderately inexpensive. Although cast iron has a lower melting point than copper, it may not last as long as the more expensive copper material fire pits.

COPPER FIRE PIT: Since copper has a very high melting point, it is considered a higher-end material for a fire pit. It is more durable than other types, is long lasting, and comes in many styles and designs.

CHIMINEA FIRE PIT: This fire pit is taller than wide. The chiminea comes in many styles and materials. The most popular materials are various metals and terracotta.

SIMPLE STONE FIRE PIT: This basic fire pit can be made by building a fire in a depression on the ground as long as it is on non-flammable dirt, soil or gravel. Also, create a ring of stones by setting them on the edges of the depression to prevent the burning logs from rolling out. By adding a grill grate and arranging the stones accordingly, it is easy to create a grilling station in the fire pit with minimal effort.

TEMPORARY OR PERMANENT STONE FIRE PIT: A stone, brick or cinderblock fire pit can be built with a little additional planning and creativity. This style of fire pit can be a permanent feature in your backyard to always enjoy.

HEAVY-DUTY STAINLESS STEEL TUB: A very inexpensive, lightweight and fireproof way to have a fire pit. Do not burn on a debris-covered area; make sure the ground is dry and non-flammable. The galvanized tub can also be used on a sandy beach or upon flat, snow-covered ground.

Fire Building

TYPES OF FIREWOOD

SOFT FIREWOOD: Soft firewood such as pine and juniper are all right to start a fire with, as they create a quick, hot blaze. Continuing to burn these types of wood is not a good idea, though, as the scents are very strong and will affect your food as it cooks. Ideally, use these soft woods only to start the fire, then add hardwoods to keep the fire going at a slow, hot, and steady burn while cooking.

DRY, HARD FIREWOOD: The best material to burn is dried wood or non-living green wood with branches. Fruitwoods such as apple, almond and cherry give off a sweet aroma and add flavor to the food. Oak is a harder wood that burns hot and long, which is perfect for cooking in a fire pit. Woods such as hickory and mesquite provide a stronger smoky flavor that complements meat and poultry very well.

TIPS AND TRICKS

The heat that emanates from embers and coals is great for cooking. The best strategy is to build a fire that burns strong and continuously for at least an hour, letting it burn down to a point where a solid foundation of hot embers is formed. This will provide a consistent base of heat.

To isolate the coals or embers, separate them with a fireplace shovel to one side of the fire pit, while a small fire continues to burn on the other. Continuously add kindling and small logs to the little fire, and move the embers aside as they are created. Also keep the coals circulating if cooking something on top of the coals, by pushing fresh hot embers underneath the pot or pan occasionally.

Never cook over an open flame, because the heat is inconsistent and there is a far greater chance of burning the outside of your food before the inside is cooked.

Avoid using chemical fire starters such as kerosene and lighter fluid. To start a fire, use only matches and long-stemmed utility lighters.

Never position a fire pit on a wooden deck or directly on top of the lawn. A stone, tile, or concrete patio is the safest spot, although a gravel surface or grass-free dry ground are easy alternatives. Once a spot is considered, make sure the fire pit is at least 10 feet from the house and that there is nothing flammable overhead.

If the ground or inside of the fire pit is wet, lay down a base of large logs on the bottom. Create a fire of additional logs and sticks on top of the base logs so the fire catches, off the wet surface.

HOW TO BUILD A WOOD COOKING FIRE

Three types and sizes of material are needed to build a good cooking fire: tinder, kindling, and firewood.

TINDER: Tinder is generally a dry, flammable material that ignites quickly with only a few sparks from a match or long-necked lighter. Materials commonly used for tinder include newspaper, dried leaves or brush, cardboard, and small dry twigs and wood pieces. Tinder is placed inside the fire pit first, with the kindling laid on top as it burns.

KINDLING: Ideally, thinly chipped firewood, small tree branches, and slightly larger dried twigs are perfect kindling for a fire pit. The trick is to make sure there is enough kindling to burn long enough that it continues to feed the flames needed to catch larger pieces of dried wood on fire.

Oxygen circulating around and through the wood is key to a good fire. Begin with the tinder and kindling. Build the dry wood on top by propping and stacking it in a crisscross fashion, making a teepee or crisscross structure. This structure uses minimal wood packed together for optimal oxygen flow.

Another method for building a fire is arranging the tinder between the kindling and larger wood, then lighting the tinder. As the fire burns, slowly add more kindling to the base of the firewood stack, until the dry wood burns well on its own.

To maintain the fire, occasionally add more firewood onto the burning logs. Allow the wood to burn down to embers while still maintaining a consistent hot fire. Split the fire in two halves of the pit, so that one side houses the hot embers while the other side remains a continuously burning fire.

A wood fire stays hot for quite a long time. Be sure to allow time in your schedule for properly dousing the flames and cooling all of the coals and embers. Do not leave a hot fire pit unattended.

Fire Pit Tools

SWEET STICK

"Sweet stick" is what I like to call the bread and biscuit stick made by Rome Industries. As many campers know, it is the perfect way to make buttermilk biscuits or crescent-roll twists, but it is also ideal for making pretzel and pizza twists. By twisting the dough around the tool in a corkscrew fashion, you can have a delicious treat in a matter of minutes.

A long 1-inch-thick wooden dowel will get the same results, and it will be inexpensive and easy to find at any local hardware store. Before you cook anything on the wooden dowel, soak it in water overnight so that the wood does not burn during the cooking process. To prevent food from sticking to the dowel or sweet stick, it is very important to spray it with nonstick cooking spray prior to wrapping food around it.

GRILLING BASKET

This particular tool was created for grilling vegetables and meats while other foods are grilling. However, it can be used to cook nearly anything over a fire pit, such as stuffed French toast, quesadillas, or even a grilled green salad.

Grilling baskets are made of nonstick metal and have heat-resistant wooden handles. They range in size from small to large, but the average size is about 12 x 12 inches. The most common basket design has three levels that adjust to the

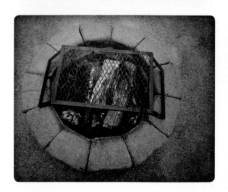

thickness of the food and a locking handle to prevent the food from falling out. Several other basket types can be found that are made specifically for grilling fish, corn on the cob, s'mores, individual meatballs, or hamburgers. Manufacturers for these products include Cuisinart, Charcoal Companion, RSVP, and others.

GRILLING GRATE

Generally found in a round or rectangular shape, grilling grates vary in sizes from 19 to 34 inches. My favorite shape is the rectangle, simply because there is space left between the long sides and the fire pit edge for tending the fire and cooking with other tools. Some grilling grates have large slotted openings that are perfect for grilling larger meats, but in my opinion, the best grates are those made with metal mesh. The smaller openings are perfect for grilling any food over the fire pit, as little to no food will fall through.

The most commonly found grilling grates are those made of stainless steel or cast iron and those with a black enamel coating. A cast-iron grilling grate is practically indestructible and can last forever if seasoned and properly cared for. Enamel-coated grates can be difficult to clean even though they are nonstick. Nearly all the types of grilling grates can be found at Wal-Mart, Home Depot, Lowe's, and most sporting goods stores, as well as online through Amazon.

You can also use the grilling grate from an old or current barbecue grill, but make sure that it fits properly over your fire pit.

PROS OF GRILLING GRATES:

⊃➜ They are simple to use and easy to clean.

⊃➜ Their slim shape does not take up much room, and some fold inward for easy storage.

⊃➜ They are very versatile and lightweight.

⊃➜ They differ in shape and size, which means you have a good chance of finding one to fit your specific fire pit.

CONS OF GRILLING GRATES:

⊃➜ They cannot be used with some fire pits, such as a chiminea.

⊃➜ They rust after a lot of use or when not protected from harsh weather.

⊃➜ They can become caked with food residue from multiple uses, especially if not cleaned properly between each use.

ALUMINUM FOIL

This kitchen staple is one of the most versatile fire pit tools. If you have a roll of heavy-duty foil and foil baking pans, you can cook nearly anything in the fire pit. Sheets of foil allow adults and children to assemble their own meal packets, and foil pans can create entrées for a whole group. The best thing about foil is that there are no dishes to clean up!

While foil is a necessary fire pit tool, there are a few disadvantages to keep in mind:

▷→ It is easy to tear and poke holes in the foil, so everything that is cooked in foil must be wrapped in multiple layers.

▷→ With multiple foil packets inside the fire pit, it can be difficult to identify which packet belongs to which person.

▷→ The ingredients need to be portioned in such a way that they all cook and are ready at the same time. For example, some ingredients such as vegetables and potatoes will take longer to cook than beef.

▷→ Food will burn and the foil will begin to fall apart if left in the fire pit longer than necessary.

TIPS FOR USING FOIL:

▷→ Only use heavy-duty foil for cooking in a fire pit. Anything less will be unsafe.

▷→ Some foods get tastier the longer they cook, such as potatoes, onions, and carrots.

▷→ For meals in packets, allow the coals in the fire pit to die down and turn white. These coals hold a consistent heat that is perfect for slow cooking. Settle the packets in between the coals and check occasionally until they reach desired doneness.

▷→ Seal the foil packets by folding the edges, not crunching it all together, to keep juices sealed in.

▷→ Foil dinners do not need to be flipped over, only rotated about halfway through the cooking process.

▷→ Always spray the inside of the foil packets with nonstick cooking spray before filling them with ingredients.

DUTCH OVEN

These heavy-duty cast-iron pots range in size from 2 quarts to 12 quarts and feature a tight-fitting lid. Pots that have little legs or feet are specifically made for cooking in the fire pit; they can sit directly on top of the hot coals. Once the pot is filled with the ingredients, shovel the hot coals on top of the lid to add circulating heat, which cooks the food more evenly. Another way to cook with a Dutch oven is to use a tripod, hanging the pot by the handle over the fire. Many dishes can be made in a Dutch oven, including soup, stew, whole chicken, braised meat, cake, bread, and much more.

IRON SANDWICH MAKER

This particular tool is known by many names, such as Pie Iron, pudgy pie, and mountain pie maker. The most common recipes for the iron sandwich maker are apple, blueberry, and other variations of dessert pies. However, many fellow campers and fire pit enthusiasts have become far more creative in making new recipes for savory and sweet pies as well as sandwiches.

The iron sandwich maker is made up of two iron castings that hook together with a hinge that is attached to two metal rods with wooden handles. Generally, this tool measures 28 inches in length and is made in a round, square, or rectangular shape. Iron sandwich makers can be found anywhere that sells camping or outdoor gear, such as Dick's Sporting Goods, Bass Pro Shop, Cabela's, and Gander Mountain. This tool can also be purchased online through camp-supply websites or Amazon.

The most commonly found producers of the iron sandwich maker are Rome Industries (Pie Iron), Texsport, Old

Mountain, and Camp Chef. While the tool is usually made of cast iron, Coleman, Palmer, and Alumna Cooker also manufacture it in aluminum. The aluminum produces a different taste and texture from the cast-iron model, but many people like this material equally as much. I prefer the cast-iron sandwich makers simply because they are all I have ever used, and they have never warped or tarnished in the 15 years I have had them. A very important tip for using this tool, whether cast iron or aluminum, is to always spray the inside of the molds with nonstick cooking spray (or grease them with butter) so that the food does not stick.

TERRA-COTTA POTS

These pots can be found in nearly any hardware store and in most craft stores or garden sections as well. They are a very inexpensive and creative way to cook inside a fire pit.

Prior to cooking anything in the pots, you should completely submerge them in water and allow to soak for 30 minutes to 1 hour. Spray the insides with nonstick cooking spray, and then line them with heavy-duty aluminum foil or parchment paper. (Alternatively, coat the insides with olive oil before lining them.) Spray the foil or parchment with cooking spray.

Before adding food to the pots, it is important to heat them gently over a low fire inside the fire pit (or in the oven at 350 for 20 minutes; heating over the fire will not take this long). This will help prevent the pots from cracking when added to the high heat of the fire for cooking. Hold the pots over the fire with fire tongs, and rotate slowly to create even heat over the entire surface. The more you use the pots, the better they will season.

TARTS ON FIRE

The Tarts on Fire stick is a very inventive and fun tool created by parents who were looking for a safer way for their kids to cook over the fire pit. A father and his son went on many camping trips where they would use sticks and dowel rods to cook biscuits over the fire. Those sticks would burn easily if they were unable to be soaked in water, and they were often too easily tossed into the flames. To solve those problems, this little mom-and-pop shop created a stainless-steel tool. It is nonstick and cleans easily, it does not need to be soaked, and little boys tend not to throw it in the fire. The cup-shaped end is perfect for making your own individual tart shells using biscuit dough, marshmallows, phyllo dough, and more. Thank you to the Tarts on Fire family for creating this tool, which can be purchased on their website at *www.tartsonfire.com.*

At Sunrise

Carb lovers

Donut Grilled Cheese Breakfast Sandwich | 17

French Toast Breakfast Wrap | 18

Caramel Sticky Buns | 21

Raspberry Cream-Stuffed French Toast | 22

Blackberry Maple Breakfast Bake | 24

Energy Booster

Everything Bagel Breakfast Sandwich | 25

Breakfast Potpies | 26

Breakfast Biscuit Cups | 28

Good Morning Skillet | 29

Donut Grilled Cheese Breakfast Sandwich

SERVES 2

Preparation time: 2 to 3 minutes

Cooking time: 4 to 8 minutes

3 glazed donuts (day-old preferred), halved

2 eggs

4 thick slices bacon, cooked and halved crosswise

1/2 cup shredded cheddar cheese

> ⊏→ Try a turkey or beef sausage patty instead of bacon.

Place 2 sandwich makers (or 1 double sandwich maker) inside the fire pit to preheat. Once the irons are heated through, open on a safe surface and spray the inside of the molds with nonstick cooking spray.

Lay 1 donut slice (glazed side down) inside one of the molds. Crack 1 egg on top of the donut slice so that it seeps down into the donut hole. Lay 4 half slices of bacon and 1 donut slice on top of the egg. Top with 1/4 cup cheddar cheese and a final donut slice (glazed side up). Repeat with the other iron.

Close the sandwich maker, making sure the sides line up and no filling escapes. Place them flat inside the fire pit on top of the hot coals. Occasionally rotate the irons so that the donut sandwich cooks evenly, 2 to 4 minutes per side. The donut will be crispy and golden brown and the egg cooked through. Remove the hot irons from the fire. Carefully open the iron, flip the sandwich onto a plate, and serve.

French Toast Breakfast Wrap

MAKES 4 WRAPS

Preparation time: 5 minutes

Cooking time: 10 to 12 minutes

2 large eggs

1 teaspoon vanilla

2 teaspoons cinnamon

$1/2$–$3/4$ cup milk

4 links maple breakfast sausage

4 slices multigrain bread, or 4 frozen multigrain waffles, thawed

Maple syrup, for serving

In a small bowl, whisk together the eggs, vanilla, cinnamon, and milk. Set aside.

Skewer the sausage links onto roasting forks and hold them over the hot coals in the fire pit. The sausage will begin to bubble up and turn a dark brown when cooked through, about 6 to 7 minutes. Remove the forks from the fire, and then carefully transfer the sausages to a plate.

Gently dip both sides of 1 slice of bread in the egg mixture, and then wrap the bread around 1 sausage. Repeat with the remaining bread and sausage. Carefully skewer the wrapped sausages back onto the forks, making sure the sealed side is facing toward the handle. Hold the forks over the hot coals for roughly 4 to 5 minutes, rotating occasionally so that the French toast turns golden brown on all sides. Once the French toast has reached the desired doneness, remove the forks from the fire pit and cautiously pull the wraps from the skewer. Serve hot with maple syrup and enjoy!

Caramel Sticky Buns

MAKES 8 BUNS

Preparation time: 10 minutes

Cooking time: 20 to 30 minutes

TOPPING

$^1/_4$ cup butter, melted

$^1/_4$ cup firmly packed brown sugar

2 tablespoons light corn syrup

$^1/_4$ cup chopped pecans

BUNS

3 tablespoons butter, melted

$^1/_3$ cup granulated sugar

$^1/_2$ teaspoon ground cinnamon

1 can grand/jumbo buttermilk biscuits
(8 count)

To make the topping, mix the melted butter, brown sugar, and corn syrup in an ungreased 8-inch foil pie pan. Sprinkle the chopped pecans on top.

To make the buns, place 3 tablespoons of melted butter in a small bowl. In another small bowl, mix the sugar and cinnamon together.

Separate the individual biscuits. Dip each biscuit into the melted butter, coating all sides. Then dip each biscuit into the sugar mixture, coating well. Arrange the biscuits with sides touching inside the pan atop the caramel topping.

Lay out 4 sheets of heavy-duty aluminum foil upon one another in a star fashion. Place the biscuit-filled pie pan in the center. Cover the filled pie pan with an empty pie pan to make a dome-like shape, making sure the sides match up. Wrap the foil upside down and over both pans and seal tight so that no juices run out as it bakes. Bake in the fire upon the hot embers or on a grate over the fire for 20 minutes. Flip the dome over and allow to bake for another 8 to 10 minutes; the caramel sauce will drip down onto the biscuits during this time. Remove from the fire and carefully check to see that the biscuits are golden brown. Allow the buns to cool for 2 minutes, then unwrap the foil, remove the top pie pan, and turn the bottom pan upside down onto a plate. Allow the sticky buns to sit for 1 minute so that the caramel drizzles downward. Serve warm.

Raspberry Cream-Stuffed French Toast

SERVES 6 TO 8

Preparation time: 15 minutes

Cooking time: 12 to 20 minutes

FILLING

8 ounces cream cheese, softened

2 tablespoons honey

2 tablespoons confectioner's sugar

1 pint (2 cups) fresh raspberries, crushed

FRENCH TOAST

1 loaf Italian bread, thickly sliced (10 to 12 slices)

6 eggs, beaten

$3/4$ cup milk

1 teaspoon vanilla

$1/4$ teaspoon cinnamon

Confectioner's sugar, for dusting

To make the filling, mix the cream cheese, honey, confectioner's sugar, and raspberries in a small bowl. Set aside.

To make the French toast, use a paring knife to cut a horizontal pocket into each slice of bread. Begin on one side of the bread and cut into the crust a little over halfway through to the other side. Make sure not to cut the entire way through. Evenly distribute the filling inside the pockets.

Whisk together the eggs, milk, vanilla, and cinnamon in a medium bowl. Lay the grilling basket open on top of a few layers of paper towels and spray the inside with non-stick cooking spray. Gently dip the filled bread slices into the egg mixture, and then place them inside the grilling basket. Roughly 6 pockets will fit at a time. Carefully close the basket to seal them in and grill over the hot coals in the fire pit for 3 to 5 minutes per side. The French toast will be golden brown and crispy on both sides. Repeat this process with the remaining slices. Dust the French toast with confectioner's sugar and serve immediately.

Carb lovers ·23

Blackberry Maple Breakfast Bake

SERVES 8

Preparation time: 15 minutes

Cooking time: 25 to 30 minutes

1 loaf rustic Tuscany or sourdough bread, cut into 1-inch cubes, divided

2 cups fresh or frozen blackberries (if using frozen, defrost and drain), divided

4 ounces mascarpone cheese, softened

$3/4$ cup egg whites, or 8 whole eggs

$1 1/2$ cups milk

$1/4$ cup maple syrup, plus more for serving

$1/4$ cup unsalted butter, melted

> ☞ Don't limit yourself to blackberries for this recipe. Try bananas, strawberries, or a combination of all three.

Spray the inside of an 8-inch-square foil pan with nonstick cooking spray. Spread half of the bread cubes in the bottom of the pan. Arrange 1 cup of the blackberries on top of the bread. Scatter the mascarpone cheese in teaspoon amounts over the bread and blackberries. Top with the remaining bread cubes and 1 cup blackberries.

In a large bowl, mix the eggs, milk, maple syrup, and melted butter. Pour the mixture evenly over the layers. Stack 4 large sheets of heavy-duty aluminum foil, and place the foil pan in the middle. Wrap and cover the pan in a tent-like shape, making sure that the top is sealed so that nothing escapes during the cooking process. Curl opposite sides inward.

Place the foil pan flat inside the fire pit on top of the hot coals or on a grill grate. Allow the breakfast dish to bake for 25 to 30 minutes, until a knife inserted in the center comes out clean.

Once the breakfast dish is baked through, take it off the fire and allow it to rest for 10 minutes before serving. Cut the dish into squares and serve with maple syrup.

Everything Bagel Breakfast Sandwich

MAKES 2 SERVINGS

Preparation time: 2 to 3 minutes

Cooking time: 6 to 8 minutes

2 everything bagels, halved

2 large eggs

2 slices muenster cheese

4 slices Roma tomatoes

3 slices bacon, cooked and halved crosswise

Place 2 sandwich makers (or 1 if double sandwich maker) inside the fire pit to preheat. Once the irons are heated through, open on a safe surface and spray the inside of the molds with nonstick cooking spray.

Place half of 1 bagel inside one of the molds. Crack 1 egg over the bagel so that it seeps into the middle and down the sides. Top with 1 cheese slice, 2 tomato slices, and 3 bacon halves. Place the other half of the bagel on top, and then carefully close the sandwich maker, making sure no filling pushes out. Repeat with the other sandwich maker and the remaining ingredients. Once the irons are locked in place, lay them on top of the hot coals inside the fire pit. Occasionally rotate the irons, allowing each side to cook for 3 to 4 minutes, until golden brown. Remove the hot iron from the fire. Carefully open the irons and flip the bagel sandwiches onto a plate. Allow the sandwiches to rest for 1 minute before serving.

⟹ For a sweeter start to the day, trade the everything bagels for blueberry or cinnamon raisin bagels.

Breakfast Potpies

MAKES 4 INDIVIDUAL PIES

Preparation time: 15 minutes

Cooking time: 10 to 15 minutes

1 tablespoon olive oil

$^1/_2$ small onion, chopped

1 clove garlic, minced

$^1/_2$ pound ground pork breakfast sausage

1 medium potato, diced

Large handful of fresh spinach

1 sheet frozen puff pastry, thawed

4 tablespoons shredded pepper Jack cheese

4 eggs

Salt and freshly ground black pepper

In a medium sauté pan, heat the olive oil and cook the onion and garlic until translucent. Add the sausage to the pan and cook until it is no longer pink. While the sausage browns, use a spatula to break it into smaller pieces. Remove the vegetables and the sausage from the pan and set aside. In the same pan, sauté the potatoes until tender and golden brown. Remove from the pan and set aside. Add the spinach to the pan and sauté until wilted. Remove from the pan and set aside.

Prepare 4 terra-cotta pots (see page 14) by lining the insides with a sheet of aluminum foil and spraying with nonstick cooking spray. Cut the sheet of puff pastry in half, and then cut those halves in half. Place a rectangle of puff pastry inside each of the pots, pressing around the sides and into the bottom. Leave the corners of the pastry to hang outside the pots.

Distribute the breakfast sausage evenly among the pots, followed by the potatoes. Sprinkle 1 tablespoon of cheese inside each pot. Break 1 egg into each pot and season with salt and pepper.

Wrap each pot in 1 sheet of heavy-duty foil by placing the pot in the center of the sheet and folding up two opposite ends to create a tent-like shape. Fold the other sides inward and seal tight.

Place the individual pots inside the fire pit on one side with the hot coals while the other side burns a small fire. Pack the hot coals around the pots, leaving room in between them for even baking. Allow the pots to bake for 5 to 7 minutes, occasionally rotating the pots with fire pit tongs. The baking time will vary depending on how hot the coals are, but be careful not to overcook. To check for doneness, remove a pot from the fire and carefully unwrap. The pastry should be crispy and brown and the egg fully cooked. Immediately remove the pots from the fire when ready. Allow to cool for 2 minutes before serving. Be careful, the pots will be hot. The potpies can be eaten right from the pots or pulled from them and served on plates.

Breakfast Biscuit Cups

MAKES 8 BISCUIT CUPS

Preparation time: 10 minutes

Cooking time: 3 to 5 minutes per biscuit

1 can grands/jumbo buttermilk biscuits (8 count)

8 large eggs, scrambled and kept warm

4 strips turkey bacon, cooked and chopped

1 cup feta cheese crumbles

Using a Tarts on Fire tool, wrap 1 biscuit in a cup-like shape around the mold. Hold the tool over the hot coals and slowly rotate for 3 to 5 minutes, until the biscuit turns golden brown and puffs up. Remove the biscuit from the fire and place it on a plate. Repeat the process with the remaining biscuits.

Fill the biscuits with layers of warm scrambled eggs, bacon pieces, and feta cheese. Serve immediately.

Good Morning Skillet

SERVES 6

Preparation time: 5 minutes

Cooking time: 12 to 15 minutes

3/4 pound maple bacon slices, roughly chopped

1 medium onion, chopped

1 (30-ounce) package frozen shredded hash brown potatoes, thawed

8 large eggs

1/2 teaspoon kosher salt

1/4 teaspoon freshly ground black pepper

1 cup shredded sharp cheddar cheese

> *For an even heartier meal, add ground maple sausage and fresh spinach leaves to the skillet.*

Set the skillet on a grill grate or directly on the coals. Cook the bacon and onion in a large cast-iron skillet. Once the bacon is crispy, drain the grease and reserve 1/4 cup of the drippings in the pan. Stir in the hash browns, and cook uncovered for 6 to 8 minutes, until the bottom is golden brown. Toss the hash brown mixture. With the back of a spoon, make 8 evenly spaced wells in the hash brown mixture. Break 1 egg into each well and sprinkle with salt and pepper. Cover the skillet loosely with aluminum foil, and allow the eggs to cook to desired doneness. Remove the foil and sprinkle with cheese. Once the cheese has melted, remove the skillet from the fire pit and serve immediately.

Apps Apps and More Apps

With a Fork

Crispy Wonton Mozzarella Sticks | 31

Spinach and Sun-Dried Tomato Pinwheels | 32

Bacon-Wrapped Scallops with Sweet
Orange Chili Dipping Sauce | 34

Mini Sweet Peppers Stuffed
with Herbed Goat Cheese | 36

Mini Fire-Pit Sandwiches | 38

In A Basket

Fire Pit Fries | 39

Flame-Grilled Buffalo Chicken Quesadilla | 40

Grilled Caesar Salad | 41

On A Stick

Pretzel Twists with Beer Cheese Sauce | 42

Pizza Twists with Marinara Sauce | 44

Anything In Between

Crab-Stuffed Portobello Mushrooms | 46

Grilled Watermelon Salad | 48

Fire-Roasted Tomato and Feta Salad | 48

Fire-Grilled Potato Salad | 49

Cheesy Prosciutto Pull-Apart Bread | 50

Ember-Roasted Eggplant, Onion,
and Garlic Dip | 52

Fire-Cooked Meatballs with Broccoli Mashed
Potato Cups | 53

Crispy Wonton Mozzarella Sticks

MAKES 8 STICKS

Preparation time: 15 minutes

Cooking time: 5 to 6 minutes

1 large egg, beaten

1 tablespoon water

8 wonton wrappers

4 pieces mozzarella string cheese, halved

½ cup marinara sauce, for serving

In a small bowl, whisk together the egg and water. Brush the edges of a wonton wrapper with the egg wash, and then place 1 piece of string cheese in the middle. Bring the bottom edge of the wrapper tightly over the cheese. Roll the wrapper over like a jelly roll, and make sure the edges are sealed shut. Repeat the process with the remaining 7 wrappers and 7 pieces of string cheese.

Gently skewer the wrapped mozzarella horizontally onto roasting forks. Cook the sticks over hot coals in the fire pit for 5 to 6 minutes, rotating occasionally, until the wrapper becomes puffy and turns golden brown. Serve with the marinara sauce.

═ VARIATION ═

For pizza lovers, add pepperoni slices inside with the mozzarella to create pizza sticks. For seafood lovers, replace the mozzarella with pre-cooked shrimp and serve with a Sweet Orange Chili Dipping Sauce (page 34) or honey mustard sauce

Spinach and Sun-Dried Tomato Pinwheels

SERVES 8

Preparation time: 50 minutes, plus 30 minutes for thawing pastry

Cooking time: 5 to 7 minutes

8 ounces frozen chopped spinach

1/4 cup sun-dried tomatoes in oil

1/4 cup mayonnaise

1/4 cup grated Parmesan cheese

1/2 teaspoon onion powder

1/2 teaspoon garlic powder

1/4 teaspoon freshly ground black pepper

1 sheet frozen puff pastry

Drain the spinach well, squeezing out moisture and pressing between layers of paper towels. Stir together the spinach, sun-dried tomatoes, mayonnaise, Parmesan, onion powder, garlic powder, and pepper. Cover and refrigerate until ready to use.

Thaw the puff pastry at room temperature for 30 minutes, or until defrosted and easy to unfold. Unfold the pastry sheet, leaving a 1/2-inch border. Spread the spinach mixture over the pastry sheet. Roll up the pastry in jelly-roll fashion, pressing to seal the seam. Wrap tightly in plastic wrap. Freeze the pinwheel logs for 30 minutes.

Cut the logs into 1/2-inch-thick slices and skewer onto roasting forks. Cook the slices over the flames in the fire pit, rotating occasionally to brown evenly. The pinwheels will puff up and turn golden brown on all sides when cooked through, about 2 to 3 minutes. Serve warm.

═VARIATIONS═

BBQ CHICKEN PINWHEELS: Mix together 1/4 cup
BBQ sauce, 1/2 cup shredded cheddar cheese, 1/4 cup cooked
and shredded chicken, 1/4 cup finely chopped red onion, and 1 1/2
tablespoons minced fresh cilantro leaves.

JALAPEÑO POPPER PINWHEELS: Mix together
6 ounces softened cream cheese, 1/2 cup shredded Mexican
cheese blend, 1 clove garlic (minced), and 1/2 cup seeded and diced
jalapeños.

Bacon-Wrapped Scallops with Sweet Orange Chili Dipping Sauce

SERVES 4

Preparation time: 15 minutes

Cooking time: 5 to 8 minutes

¹/₄ pound lean bacon, halved or cut into thirds

1 pound large sea scallops

Sweet Orange Chili Dipping Sauce (recipe below)

To make the scallops, wrap the bacon pieces around the outside of the scallops. Slide 2 wrapped scallops onto each roasting fork, leaving a small amount of space between them. Gently cook over the hot coals in the fire pit for 5 to 8 minutes, making sure to rotate occasionally for even doneness. The bacon will crisp up and turn golden brown, and the scallops will begin to split. Remove the scallops from the fire and serve with the sweet orange chili dipping sauce.

SWEET ORANGE CHILI DIPPING SAUCE

³/₄ tablespoon cornstarch

¹/₄ cup water

³/₄ cup orange marmalade

3 cloves garlic

2 red chili peppers, stemmed and seeded

3 tablespoons rice vinegar

1 tablespoon honey

1 tablespoon Thai red chili paste

Juice of ¹/₂ lemon

To make the sauce, mix the cornstarch and water in a small bowl. Set aside. In a food processor, puree the marmalade, garlic, peppers, rice vinegar, honey, chili paste, and lemon juice. Transfer the puree into a small saucepan and bring to a boil over medium-high heat. Allow the mixture to simmer for 4 minutes. Stir in the cornstarch paste and simmer for 1 minute. The sauce will thicken and turn glossy. Remove the sauce from the heat, and allow it to cool completely. Transfer the sauce to a container and refrigerate.

Mini Sweet Peppers Stuffed with Herbed Goat Cheese

MAKES 5 TO 6 SERVINGS

Preparation time: 5 minutes

Cooking time: 3 to 4 minutes

10 mini sweet peppers, stems and cores removed

4 ounces herbed goat cheese

These mini peppers can be made ahead of time and chilled in the refrigerator until ready to cook.

Stuff the mini sweet peppers with the herbed goat cheese until it reaches the top of the pepper. Skewer 2 to 3 of the stuffed peppers onto a roasting fork, leaving enough space between them for even cooking. Gently hold the sweet peppers above the hot coals and low flames so the skin begins to blacken and turn crispy. Rotating the peppers side to side will help prevent the melted cheese from leaking out during cooking.

Once the peppers have become crispy and somewhat blackened, remove from the fire pit and allow them to cool for 1 minute. Eat warm.

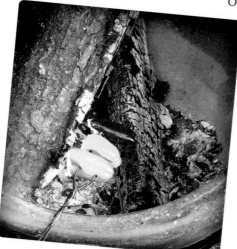

Mini Fire-Pit Sandwiches

MAKES 8 MINI SANDWICHES

Preparation time: 3 minutes

Cooking time: 2 to 3 minutes

1/2 baguette, halved lengthwise and cut into 1/2-inch pieces

2 slices oven-roasted turkey breast (deli meat), halved

2 slices off-the-bone ham (deli meat), halved

2 slices provolone cheese, halved

2 slices Land O' Lakes American cheese, halved

8 pickles

8 cherry tomatoes

Mayonnaise, for serving

Brown mustard, for serving

Skewer 1 piece of baguette followed by 1 piece of deli meat, 1 piece of cheese, 1 pickle, and 1 cherry tomato, finishing with a second piece of baguette. Make sure to leave space between the items so that everything cooks properly. Hold the skewers over the fire pit for 2 to 3 minutes, rotating occasionally. The sandwiches are ready when the cheese begins to melt and the bread is toasted. Slide the mini sandwiches off the skewers and onto a plate. Top with mayonnaise or mustard (or both) and serve immediately.

Fire Pit Fries

SERVES 4

Preparation time: 10 minutes

Cooking time: 25 to 30 minutes

2 sweet potatoes, sliced into 1/2-inch-thick wedges

Kosher salt

Freshly ground black pepper

Garlic powder

1 tablespoon olive oil

1/2 teaspoon fresh thyme leaves

☞ Try these fries loaded with toppings: mixed shredded cheeses, chopped bacon or chives, chili, sour cream, barbecue sauce, ground meat, or anything else your heart desires.

Spray a grilling basket with nonstick cooking spray and set aside. Place the sweet potato wedges in a large bowl. Season with kosher salt, pepper, and garlic powder; then toss with the olive oil and thyme leaves. After coating the wedges, arrange them inside the grilling basket. Be sure not to smash the wedges down inside the basket; leave enough space to toss the wedges as they cook.

Hold the grilling basket over the hot embers, and allow the sweet potato wedges to cook for 15 minutes on one side. Gently rotate to allow the other side to cook for an additional 10 to 15 minutes. Occasionally shake the basket to toss and separate the wedges, which will provide a more even bake. Watch them closely to ensure they do not burn. The wedges are ready when they turn crispy and golden brown. Allow them to cool slightly, then serve with your favorite sauce.

Flame-Grilled Buffalo Chicken Quesadilla

SERVES 6

Preparation time: 15 minutes

Cooking time: 10 to 16 minutes

2 cups shredded cooked chicken

4 tablespoons Frank's RedHot Buffalo Wings Sauce

2 tablespoons freshly squeezed lemon juice

$1/4$ cup thinly sliced celery

$1/2$ small red onion, thinly sliced

2 large flour tortillas

2 cups shredded Mexican cheese blend, divided

$1/2$ cup crumbled blue cheese

Sour cream, for serving

Chopped fresh parsley, for serving

Spray the inside of 2 grilling baskets with non-stick cooking spray. Set aside. Mix the chicken, wing sauce, lemon juice, celery, and onion in a bowl. Lay 1 tortilla on a flat surface. Spread half of the chicken mixture over one half of the tortilla, making sure to leave a $1/2$-inch border around the outside edge. Sprinkle 1 cup of the Mexican cheese blend and $1/4$ cup of the blue cheese on top. Gently fold the other half of the flour tortilla over the filling. Prepare a second quesadilla with the remaining tortilla, chicken mixture, 1 cup Mexican cheese blend, and $1/4$ cup blue cheese. Lay the quesadillas inside the grilling baskets, adjusting as needed so that they stay snug while cooking.

Hold the grilling baskets over the hot embers with the exposed filling side facing slightly upward so that no filling escapes. Cook the quesadillas for 5 to 8 minutes per side, occasionally rotating the basket to ensure even cooking. The quesadilla will be bubbling inside and turn golden brown outside when cooked through. Slice the quesadillas into thirds and serve with sour cream and parsley.

Grilled Caesar Salad

SERVES 2 TO 4

Preparation time: 5 minutes

Cooking time: 3 to 6 minutes

2 slices crusty bread (such as a baguette)

2 tablespoons olive oil, divided

2 heads baby romaine hearts, halved lengthwise

Salt and freshly ground black pepper

$1/2$ cup Caesar dressing

Shaved Parmesan cheese

Brush both sides of the bread with 1 tablespoon of the olive oil, and place them in a grilling basket over the hot fire pit. Toast the bread on both sides until it starts to char on the edges, about 1 to 2 minutes. Remove the bread from the basket and set aside on a plate.

Brush the outsides of the romaine with the remaining 1 tablespoon olive oil. Place the romaine inside the grilling basket and grill cut side down over the fire pit for 2 to 3 minutes, just until the lettuce starts to wilt. Transfer the romaine to a plate, season with salt and pepper, and drizzle with the Caesar dressing. Sprinkle the Parmesan on top and serve immediately with the toasted bread.

> ➡ For a livelier salad, add 3 strips of crispy bacon and $2^1/2$ ounces of crumbled blue cheese to the grilled romaine. Replace the Caesar dressing with a mixture of 1 tablespoon each of olive oil, balsamic vinegar, and Worcestershire sauce.

Pretzel Twists with Beer Cheese Sauce

MAKES UP TO 4 TWISTS

Preparation time: 15 minutes, plus 1 to 8 hours for thawing dough

Cooking time: 12 to 15 minutes

1 package frozen dinner rolls (such as Rhodes; not prebaked rolls)

1 large egg yolk

1 tablespoon water

$\frac{2}{3}$ cup baking soda

10 cups hot water

Pinch of coarse sea salt or pretzel salt

Beer Cheese Sauce (recipe follows)

The night before you make the twists, thaw the number of rolls you wish to use (1 roll makes 1 twist) according to the package directions.

In a small bowl, whisk together the egg and water. Set aside.

Line a cookie sheet with parchment paper and spray with nonstick cooking spray. Roll the length of each dough into a 12- to 15-inch rope and place on the cookie sheet. In a large bowl, dissolve the baking soda in hot water. Holding the ends of 1 rope, dip it into the hot water and baking soda mix for 30 seconds. Place the dipped rope back on the cookie sheet. Repeat with the remaining ropes.

Spray sweet sticks (see page 10) or wooden dowels with non-stick cooking spray. To form the pretzel twist, wrap the dough around the stick in a corkscrew fashion, beginning at the very end of the stick and making sure the dough just touches as it is wrapped around. Tuck the end of the rope under the previous wrap of dough so that it does not come uncurled while baking. Brush the twist with the egg wash and sprinkle with salt. Cook the twist over the fire for about 10 to 12 minutes, rotating to produce an even color. Pretzels will be dark golden brown when cooked through. Serve warm with beer cheese sauce.

BEER CHEESE SAUCE

MAKES 2 CUPS

Preparation time: 10 minutes

Cooking time: 20 minutes

2 tablespoons unsalted butter

2 tablespoons flour

1 (12 ounces) dark beer or ale (a Yuengling Black and Tan or a Rogue Dead Guy ale)

1 teaspoon dry mustard

2 teaspoons Worcestershire sauce

Dash of cayenne

8 ounces sharp cheddar cheese, freshly shredded

2 ounces fontina cheese, freshly grated

Salt and freshly ground black pepper

Melt the butter in a saucepan over medium heat. Add the flour and whisk continuously for 3 to 4 minutes, until the mixture is smooth and tan in color. Add the beer and bring to a simmer, whisking continuously. Add the dry mustard, Worcestershire sauce, and cayenne; continue whisking until the mixture thickens, roughly 3 minutes.

Add the cheddar and fontina cheeses in 3 parts, making sure the cheese melts completely each time before adding more. Season the sauce to taste with salt and pepper and serve warm.

⊃➧ *Try using a pumpkin beer (like Samuel Adams Pumpkin Patch) instead of a dark ale for a fall flavored upgrade.*

Pizza Twists with Marinara Sauce

MAKES 4 TWISTS

Preparation time: 10 to 12 minutes

Cooking time: 10 to 15 minutes

1 (13.8-ounce) can refrigerated pizza dough

$1/2$ teaspoon dried basil

$1/2$ teaspoon dried parsley

$1/2$ teaspoon garlic powder

$3/4$ cup shredded mozzarella cheese

$1/2$ cup pepperoni slices

2 tablespoons butter, melted

1 tablespoon grated Parmesan cheese

Marinara sauce or pizza sauce, for serving

Unroll the pizza dough and cut into 4 rectangles roughly 2 inches wide by 5 inches long. Sprinkle the basil, parsley, and garlic powder over the dough. Top the rectangles with mozzarella and pepperoni, distributing evenly. Gently twist each rectangle and pinch the ends. Brush the melted butter over each twist.

Spray sweet sticks (see page 10) or wooden dowels with non-stick cooking spray. Wrap the dough around the stick in a corkscrew fashion, beginning at the very end of the stick and making sure the dough just touches as it is wrapped around. Tuck the end of the rope under the previous wrap of dough so that it does not come uncurled while baking. Sprinkle the twist with Parmesan before cooking over the hot coals in the fire pit. Slowly rotate the twist for 10 to 15 minutes to allow for an even, crispy bake and golden brown color. Serve with warm marinara sauce or pizza sauce.

Crab-Stuffed Portobello Mushrooms

SERVES 6

Preparation time: 15 minutes

Cooking time: 7 to 11 minutes

6 portobello mushrooms

Pinch of sea salt

Pinch of freshly ground black pepper

8 ounces lump crabmeat

1 egg, lightly beaten

$1/2$ cup panko breadcrumbs

2 tablespoons finely chopped sweet onion

2 cloves minced garlic

1 tbsp dry thyme

Juice of $1/2$ lemon (about $1 1/2$ tablespoons)

$1/2$ cup coarsely grated Gruyère cheese

Lemon wedges, for serving

Remove the stems from the mushroom caps. Finely chop the stems, place them in a mixing bowl, and set aside. Remove the mushroom gills by scraping the caps with a teaspoon, then gently brush the caps clean. Spray a 9-inch-round foil pan with nonstick cooking spray, and arrange the mushroom caps inside the pan. Season the mushrooms with salt and pepper and set aside.

Add the crabmeat, egg, breadcrumbs, onions, garlic, thyme, and lemon juice to the chopped portobello stems. Gently combine all the ingredients and evenly distribute the stuffing mixture into the mushroom caps. Gently compress the stuffing to form a slight mound on top of each mushroom. Evenly distribute the Gruyère cheese on top of the stuffed mushrooms and press down gently again.

Stack 4 large sheets of heavy-duty aluminum foil, place the pan in the middle, and bring the longer ends of the foil up into a tent-like shape. Fold the foil down, then seal in the opposite sides by curling them inward and under the edges so no steam escapes during the cooking process. Place the pan flat inside the fire pit on top of the hot coals or on top of a grill grate. Allow the mushrooms to cook until the crab stuffing is a light golden brown. Check the mushrooms after 7 minutes; if more time is needed, cook for an additional 3 to 4 minutes. Serve warm with lemon wedges.

Grilled Watermelon Salad

SERVES 4 TO 6

Preparation time: 6 to 8 minutes

Cook time: 3 to 6 minutes

1 small seedless watermelon

1 tablespoon olive oil

Juice and zest of 1 lemon

2 fresh basil leaves, torn

4 fresh mint leaves, torn

$^1/_2$ cup shaved Parmesan cheese

Cut the watermelon into $^1/_2$-inch thick slices, and then cut the slices into triangle-shaped quarters. Brush the watermelon slices with the olive oil on both sides. Arrange a single layer of slices inside a grilling basket and cook for 2 to 3 minutes per side. Remove the watermelon from the basket and set aside to cool. Repeat the process with the remaining watermelon slices. Trim the rind off each grilled slice, and cut the watermelon into chunks. Add the watermelon to a serving bowl with the lemon juice and zest, basil, mint, and Parmesan. Toss and serve.

Fire-Roasted Tomato and Feta Salad

SERVES 4

Preparation time: 10 minutes

Cook time: 5 to 7 minutes

1 cup cherry tomatoes, halved

$^1/_3$ cup chopped kalamata olives

$^1/_4$ cup thinly sliced red onion

1 clove garlic, minced

1 teaspoon olive oil

2 tablespoons chopped fresh parsley

8-10 ounces feta cheese, crumbled

Flat bread or pita chips, for serving

In a medium bowl, toss together the tomatoes, olives, red onion, garlic, olive oil, and 1 tablespoon of the parsley. Stack 4 sheets of heavy-duty aluminum foil large enough to hold and wrap around the salad. Transfer the salad to the center of the foil and sprinkle with the feta. Fold up the opposite ends of the foil to create a tent-like shape, and then fold the seams down to create a packet. Place the packet on top of the hot coals in the fire pit. Cook for 5 to 7 minutes, until the tomatoes are roasted and the cheese has melted slightly. Remove the salad from the fire pit and serve inside the foil packet with flat bread or pita chips.

Fire-Grilled Potato Salad

SERVES 3

Preparation time: 10 minutes

Cooking time: 8 to 10 minutes

Pinch of sea salt

Pinch of freshly ground black pepper

1 teaspoon red pepper flakes

1 tablespoon olive oil

5 red potatoes, quartered

1 small red onion, thinly sliced

3 1/2 tablespoons mayonnaise

1 1/2 tablespoons brown mustard

1 teaspoon Worcestershire sauce

2 tablespoons chopped fresh parsley

In a large bowl, combine the salt, pepper, red pepper flakes, and olive oil. Mix well. Toss the potatoes and red onions in the mixture, coating well. Stack 4 sheets of heavy-duty aluminum foil large enough to hold and wrap around the potato mixture. Transfer the potato mixture to the center of the foil. Fold up the opposite ends to create a tent-like shape, and then fold the seams down to create a packet. Place the potato packet inside the fire on top of the hot embers. Allow the packet to cook for 8 to 10 minutes. Check that the potatoes are tender and that they are crispy where they touch the foil. Cook longer if needed. While the potatoes cook, mix together the mayonnaise, mustard, and Worcestershire sauce. Once the potatoes are ready, transfer them from the foil packet into a bowl. Gently toss them with the mayonnaise mixture, coating well. Sprinkle the parsley on top. Serve hot or warm.

Cheesy Prosciutto Pull-Apart Bread

SERVES 6 TO 8

Preparation time: 15 minutes

Cooking time: 10 to 15 minutes

1 loaf firm rustic bread, such as country or multigrain

1/2 pound prosciutto, chopped

1/2 pint cherry tomatoes, chopped

1 tablespoon minced garlic

1/2 pound creamy Havarti cheese, diced

1/4 cup butter, melted

Using a serrated knife, cut a 1/2-inch grid pattern about three-quarters of the way into the bread, taking care not to cut all the way through.

Mix the prosciutto, cherry tomatoes, garlic, and Havarti in a bowl. Pour the melted butter over the mixture and combine. Using your hands, stuff the entire mixture into the crevices of the bread.

Stack 4 sheets of heavy-duty aluminum foil large enough to cover the stuffed loaf of bread. Wrap the foil around the loaf, making sure the edges are sealed. Place the wrapped loaf in the fire on top of the hot coals and bake for 10 to 15 minutes. Make sure to rotate the loaf so that it does not burn. You may need to add extra time, depending on how hot your coals are. Once the cheese has melted, remove the loaf from the fire and allow to cool slightly. Serve warm.

═ V A R I A T I O N S ═

HAM AND CHEESE PULL-APART BREAD: Add small chunks of ham and a cheese of your choice instead of prosciutto and Harvati.

SPINACH AND ARTICHOKE PULL-APART BREAD: Use a loaf of sourdough bread, and replace the prosciutto and tomatoes with 1 or 2 good handfuls fresh spinach, chopped, and 1 (14-ounce) can artichoke hearts, drained and chopped.

Ember-Roasted Eggplant, Onion, and Garlic Dip

MAKES 6 SERVINGS

Preparation time: 5 minutes

Cooking time: 15 to 20 minutes

3 medium eggplants (about 2 pounds total)

1 medium onion

1 bulb garlic

1/2 cup olive oil

1/2 cup plain Greek yogurt

1/4 cup freshly squeezed lemon juice

1/2 teaspoon paprika

Sea salt

Pita chips or crackers, for serving

Carefully bury the eggplants, onion, and garlic inside the hot embers of the fire pit. Allow the embers to slowly roast the vegetables for 10 to 15 minutes, until their skins turn a dark shade of brown or black and their insides become very soft. The time will vary depending on how hot the embers are. Remove the vegetables from the fire pit with tongs or fire gloves, and place them in a stainless steel bowl. Cover the bowl with plastic wrap, and allow the steam from the vegetables to soften the skins for easier removal.

Once most of the skin has pulled away from the vegetables, remove the plastic wrap and gently clean off the burnt skins. Place the insides of the vegetables in another bowl. With either a mixer or potato masher, thoroughly mix the vegetables together. Add the olive oil, Greek yogurt, lemon juice, and paprika; combine the mixture until smooth. Add sea salt to taste. Serve with pita chips or crackers.

> ⤙➔ Try sweet potatoes as a delicious alternative to eggplant. Roast the sweet potatoes for about 15 minutes, rotating every 5 to 6 minutes, until the skin is blackened and a skewer pierces the potato easily.

Fire-Cooked Meatballs with Broccoli Mashed Potato Cups

SERVES 4 TO 6

Preparation time: 30 minutes, plus overnight for the potatoes to set

Cooking time: 8 to 12 minutes

$^1/_2$ pound Yukon gold potatoes, cut into wedges

$^1/_2$ pound broccoli crowns, chopped (about 1 cup)

$^1/_2$ cup shredded fontina cheese

$^1/_4$ cup milk, warm

Kosher salt

Freshly ground black pepper

4-6 frozen precooked meatballs, thawed

Prepare the mashed potato mixture 1 day ahead. Bring 1 inch of water to a boil in a large pot. Steam the potatoes and broccoli until tender, then transfer them to a large bowl. Coarsely mash the broccoli and potatoes with the cheese and milk until creamy and smooth, adding salt and pepper to taste. Wrap the potato mixture in a sheet of plastic wrap and refrigerate overnight. When ready to use, remove from the refrigerator and bring to room temperature.

Using a Tarts on Fire tool, mold the potato mixture around the tool to create a cup-like shape. Carefully hold the tool over the hot coals in the fire pit for about 4 to 5 minutes, rotating occasionally so that the potato cup browns evenly on all sides. Gently transfer the potato cup to a plate. Heat the meatballs over the fire with fire pit forks for about 4 to 7 minutes. Repeat the process with the remaining potato mixture. Once all of the mashed potato, broccoli cups are made, place a heated meatball inside each one and serve immediately.

Major Eats

Fork Favorites

Philly Cheesesteak Hot Dogs | 55

Agave-Lime Shrimp Tacos | 56

Chili, Cheese, and Corn Chip Sweet Sausages | 58

Turkey Hot Dogs with Greek Hummus and Tzatziki | 59

Hot Sausage Enchiladas | 60

Wrapped in Foil

Autumn Pasta Bake | 61

Cajun Crab Legs and Pasta | 62

Steamed Mussels with Mustard Sauce | 63

Lemon Chicken with Artichokes | 65

Maple Chicken with Sweet Potatoes | 66

Fire-Roasted Ratatouille | 69

Iron Sandwiches

Apple, Fontina, and Spinach Quesadillas | 71

Chicken and Peach Quesadillas with Agave-Lime Sauce | 72

Spaghetti Iron Sandwich | 75

Thanksgiving Sandwich | 76

Reuben Sandwich | 77

French Onion Soup Sandwich | 78

In a Grilling Basket

Phyllo-Wrapped Salmon | 79

Cedar-Wrapped Cod with Spinach Pesto | 80

Traditional Calzone | 82

Family Style

Iron-Skillet Stuffed Cabbage | 83

Iron-Skillet Lasagna | 84

Dutch-Oven Guinness Beef Stew | 85

Mini Macaroni and Cheese Pots | 86

Bruschetta Pizza | 87

Rustic White Pizza with Scallops and Pancetta | 88

Grilled Stuffed Flank Steak | 90

Philly Cheesesteak Hot Dogs

SERVES 4

Preparation time: 5 minutes

Cooking time: 10 to 15 minutes

4 all-beef hot dogs

4 hot dog buns

$^1/_2$ pound roast beef or shredded steak, chopped, cooked

$^1/_2$ red bell pepper, chopped

$^1/_2$ orange bell pepper, chopped

1 onion, thinly sliced

4 slices provolone cheese

Skewer the hot dogs horizontally onto roasting forks and hold over the fire pit, rotating occasionally so that each side cooks evenly. Cook for 5 to 8 minutes, depending on how hot the fire is. Once the hot dogs are cooked to desired doneness, remove them from the fire and place inside the hot dog buns. Top each hot dog with the roast beef, red and orange peppers, onion, and the provolone, distributing evenly. Wrap each dressed hot dog in 2 sheets of aluminum foil, and place them inside the fire pit near the hot coals for 5 to 7 minutes. Gently rotate with tongs so that the roast beef, vegetables, and cheese heat through. When the hot dogs are ready, remove them from the fire pit, unwrap the foil, and serve hot.

≡ VARIATION ≡

BACON-WRAPPED SOUTHWESTERN HOT DOG: Wrap 1 slice of bacon around each hot dog before cooking over the fire pit. Instead of the Philly toppings, dress each hot dog with 1-2 tablespoons guacamole and 1 slice of pepper Jack cheese.

Agave-Lime Shrimp Tacos

SERVES 6 TO 8

PREPARATION TIME: 1 HOUR

COOKING TIME: 20 MINUTES FOR CORN,
3 TO 5 MINUTES FOR SHRIMP

MARINADE

$^{1}/_{4}$ cup olive oil

2 cloves garlic, minced

Juice of 1 lime

1 tablespoon agave nectar

$^{1}/_{3}$ cup tequila

Pinch of sea salt

SHRIMP

3 ears unhusked corn

1 pound large raw shrimp, peeled,
deveined, and tails removed

6-8 small flour tortillas, warmed

3 ears grilled corn, kernels reserved

2 cups shredded pepper Jack cheese

1 cup cherry tomatoes, halved

1 handful arugula

$^{1}/_{2}$ cup fresh cilantro leaves

Mix all of the marinade ingredients together in a large ziplock bag with the raw shrimp. Place the shrimp in the refrigerator to marinate for 30 minutes to 1 hour.

Meanwhile, prepare the corn for roasting by soaking the ears in water for about 30 minutes. Remove ears and drain excess water. Peel back the husks just far enough to remove the silk, then put the husks back in place as tightly as possible. Twist and/or tie the husks together at the top. Set the ears on the white coals and turn about every 5 minutes to roast all sides. Total cooking time will be about 20 minutes, depending on the heat of your fire. Carefully test for doneness by peeling down the husk and pressing on a kernel with your fingernail to see if it is tender to your liking. When cooked, cut the corn kernels from the cobs.

Skewer the shrimp onto roasting forks; 2 to 3 shrimp will fit per fork, depending on their size. Grill the shrimp over the hot coals in the fire pit until they turn pink, 3 to 5 minutes. Be careful not to overcook. Remove the grilled shrimp from the forks, and divide them evenly among the warm tortillas. Top each taco with the grilled corn kernels, pepper Jack, tomatoes, arugula, and cilantro, distributing evenly. Serve while the shrimp are still warm.

=VARIATION=

Fire-Roasted Tuna Tacos: Marinate and then grill tuna or salmon in small chunks on a roasting fork in place of the shrimp.

Chili, Cheese and Corn Chip Sweet Sausages

SERVES 4

Preparation time: 10 to 12 minutes

Cooking time: 11 to 15 minutes

4 sweet Italian sausages in casings, pre-boiled

4 long rolls

1 (15-ounce) can no-beans chili

$^1/_2$ cup shredded cheddar cheese

1 cup corn chips

Skewer the sweet sausages horizontally onto roasting forks and hold over the fire pit, rotating occasionally so that the sides cooks evenly. Cook for 8 to 10 minutes, depending on how hot the fire is and how large the sausages are. Once the sausages are cooked to desired doneness, remove them from the fire and place inside the long rolls. Top each sausage with the chili and cheddar, distributing evenly. Wrap each dressed sausage in 2 sheets of heavy-duty aluminum foil, and place them inside the fire pit near the hot coals for 3 to 5 minutes. Gently rotate with tongs so that the chili and cheddar heat through. When the sausages are ready, remove them from the fire pit, unwrap the foil, and top each one with $^1/_4$ cup corn chips. Serve immediately.

Turkey Hot Dogs with Greek Hummus and Tzatziki

SERVES 4

Preparation time: 10 minutes

Cooking time: 8 to 9 minutes

TZATZIKI

$1/2$ cup plain Greek yogurt

$1/2$ cucumber, finely chopped

1-2 teaspoons freshly squeezed lemon juice

1 clove garlic, crushed

Coarse salt

HOT DOGS

4 turkey hot dogs

$1/2$ cup hummus

4 hot dog buns

$1/2$ cup diced red bell pepper

$1/2$ cup diced yellow bell pepper

$1/2$ cup diced red onion

To make the tzatziki, mix the yogurt, cucumber, lemon juice, and garlic in a small bowl; season to taste with salt. Set aside.

Spread 2 tablespoons of the hummus inside each hot dog bun on one side. Set aside. Skewer the hot dogs horizontally onto roasting forks and hold over the fire pit, rotating occasionally so that each side cooks evenly. Cook for 5 to 8 minutes, depending on how hot the fire is. Once the hot dogs are cooked to desired doneness, remove them from the fire and place inside the hummus-lined buns. Top each hot dog with the tzatziki sauce, red and yellow peppers, and onion, distributing evenly. Serve immediately.

Hot Sausage Enchiladas

MAKES 4 SERVINGS

Preparation time: 5 minutes

Cooking time: 12 to 14 minutes

4 hot Italian sausages in casings, pre-boiled

4 (6-inch) flour tortillas

1 cup salsa

$^1/_2$ cup shredded Monterey Jack cheese

1 avocado, sliced

$^1/_2$ cup sour cream

Skewer the sausages horizontally onto roasting forks and hold over the fire pit, rotating occasionally so that each side cooks evenly. Cook for 8 to 10 minutes, depending on how hot the fire is and how large the sausages are. Once the sausages are cooked to desired doneness, remove them from the fire and place inside the flour tortillas, wrapping them up like enchiladas. Place each wrapped sausage on 2 sheets of heavy-duty aluminum foil. Top each one with 4 tablespoons of the salsa and 2 tablespoons of the Monterey Jack. Wrap the foil around the enchiladas, and place them inside the fire pit near the hot coals for 2 to 6 minutes. Gently rotate with tongs so that the salsa heats through and the cheese melts. When the enchiladas are ready, remove them from the fire pit, unwrap the foil, and top each one with avocado slices and 2 tablespoons of the sour cream. Serve immediately.

Autumn Pasta Bake

SERVES 8

Preparation time: 20 minutes

Cooking time: 25 to 35 minutes

1 (2-pound) butternut squash, peeled and cut into 1-inch cubes

1 onion, cut into $1/2$-inch-thick wedges

$1/2$ teaspoon crushed red pepper flakes

2 tablespoons olive oil

3 cups rigatoni pasta, cooked according to package directions

4 ounces cream cheese, cubed and softened

$1/4$ cup milk

$1/4$ cup panko breadcrumbs

1 (8-ounce) package triple cheddar shredded cheese

In a large mixing bowl, thoroughly combine the squash, onion, red pepper flakes, olive oil, pasta, cream cheese, and milk. Pour the mixture into a 9 x 13-inch foil pan. Top the dish with the panko breadcrumbs and cheddar.

Stack 4 large sheets of heavy-duty aluminum foil, and place the pan in the middle. Cover and wrap the foil pan tightly so that no steam or juices escape. Bake in the fire pit on top of a grill grate for 25 to 35 minutes, until the squash is tender and the cheese is golden brown. Serve warm.

Cajun Crab Legs and Pasta

SERVES 4

Preparation time: 4 to 5 minutes

Cooking time: 7 to 8 minutes

2 cups heavy cream

1 tablespoon chopped fresh basil

1 tablespoon chopped fresh thyme leaves

1/2 cup chopped fresh parsley

2 teaspoons sea salt

2 teaspoons freshly ground black pepper

1 1/2 teaspoons crushed red pepper flakes

1 cup chopped scallions

2 pounds crab legs

1 pound angel hair pasta, cooked according to package directions

1/2 cup shredded Parmigiano-Reggiano cheese

Stack 4 large sheets of heavy-duty aluminum foil and set an aluminum pie pan or cake pan on top Pour in the heavy cream and add the basil, thyme, parsley, salt, pepper, red pepper flakes, and scallions. Arrange the crab legs in the pie pan, then fold up and seal the pieces of foil to seal in the liquid and make a steam tent.

Place the foiled pan on the hot coals in the fire pit. Allow the crab legs to steam for 7 to 8 minutes, depending on how hot the coals are. Remove the pan from the fire pit, open the pouch, and toss in the pasta and cheese to heat through. Serve hot.

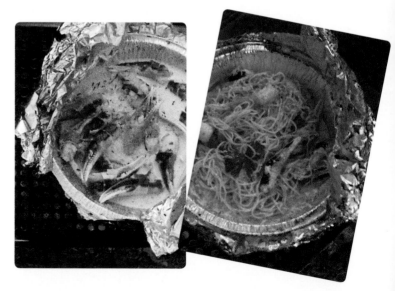

Steamed Mussels with Mustard Sauce

SERVES 3

Preparation time: 15 minutes

Cooking time: 4 to 5 minutes

1 tablespoon butter, melted

2 tablespoons finely chopped shallots

1 clove garlic, minced

1 bay leaf

$^1/_2$ teaspoon dried thyme

$^1/_4$ cup white cooking wine

$^1/_2$ cup heavy cream

2 tablespoons Dijon mustard

Pinch of freshly ground black pepper

1 teaspoon sea salt

$^3/_4$ quart mussels, cleaned, debearded, and scrubbed

2 cups prepared angel hair pasta

2 tablespoons chopped fresh flat-leaf parsley

In a 9-inch foil pie pan, combine the butter, shallots, garlic, bay leaf, thyme, wine, heavy cream, Dijon mustard, pepper, and salt. Gently toss the mussels in the sauce and seasonings. Stack 4 sheets of heavy-duty aluminum foil large enough to wrap around the foil pan and seal closed. Place the pan of mussels in the center of the foil. Fold the opposite ends of the foil together to make a tent-like shape, and seal the edges to prevent the steam and juices from escaping.

Place the pan on top of the grilling grate over the fire pit. Allow the mussels to steam for 4 to 5 minutes, rotating occasionally so that the bottom does not burn. Check the mussels by unfolding the foil. The mussels will open when cooked through, and the sauce will bubble and thicken slightly. When the mussels are ready, gently toss in the angel hair pasta and parsley to heat through. Serve hot from the foil pan.

Lemon Chicken with Artichokes

SERVES 2

Preparation time: 15 minutes

Cooking time: 15 to 20 minutes

³/₄ pound boneless chicken breasts, diced into bite-sized pieces

Sea salt and freshly cracked black pepper

1 tablespoon canola oil

1 (9-ounce) package artichoke hearts, thawed and quartered

¹/₂ lemon, thinly sliced

2-3 tablespoons white wine

¹/₂ teaspoon fresh thyme leaves

Freshly shaved Parmesan cheese, for garnish

Prepared wild rice, for serving

Season both sides of the chicken with salt and pepper. Stack 4 sheets of 12 by 12-inch heavy-duty aluminum foil. Drizzle the top sheet with the canola oil, leaving a 1- to 2-inch perimeter untouched. Place the chicken and artichoke hearts on top of the canola oil. Arrange the lemon slices on top. Mix together the white wine and thyme leaves in a small bowl, then pour over all of the ingredients in the packet.

To seal the packet, pull up the two longer ends of the foil to create a tent-like shape. Fold the ends together and downward, then curl the opposite ends inward, sealing tightly to prevent leaking.

Lay the filled packet flat on top of the hot coals or on a grill grate over the fire. Cook the packet for 15 to 20 minutes before checking. The chicken should be fully cooked and the artichokes tender. Serve immediately with wild rice and garnish with Parmesan.

Maple Chicken with Sweet Potatoes

SERVES 2

Preparation time: 10 minutes

Cooking time: 22 to 30 minutes

1 tablespoon olive oil

1 pound boneless, skinless chicken breast, cut into bite-sized pieces

$1/2$ teaspoon kosher salt

$1/8$ teaspoon freshly ground black pepper

1 medium sweet potato, peeled and cut into 1-inch cubes

$1/2$ yellow onion, cut into 1-inch wedges

2 tablespoons maple syrup

2 sprigs thyme

Stack 4 sheets of 12 x 12-inch heavy-duty aluminum foil. Drizzle the top sheet with the olive oil, leaving a 1-inch perimeter untouched. Place the chicken on top of the olive oil and season with salt and pepper. Arrange the sweet potatoes and onion wedges around the chicken. Top with the maple syrup and thyme.

To seal the packet closed, fold up two opposite sides and tightly fold over several times. Fold the foil ends down and under the foil pouch, making a packet.

Place the foil packet flat on top of the hot coals or on a grill grate over the fire. Cook for 10 to 12 minutes before flipping to cook for an additional 12 minutes. The packet will sizzle during the cooking process. To check for doneness, gently take the packet off the fire and carefully uncurl the foil. The chicken will be golden in color and the vegetables tender. If more time is needed, tightly curl the pouches closed and return to the fire. Once the chicken and vegetables are cooked through, serve immediately.

> ⟫→ For a spicy kick, add a little Dijon mustard to the packet.

Fire-Roasted Ratatouille

SERVES 4 TO 6

Preparation time: 25 minutes

Cooking time: 40 minutes

1 cup marinara sauce, divided

1 small yellow onion, thinly sliced

1 small eggplant, thinly sliced

1 medium zucchini, thinly sliced

1 medium yellow squash, thinly sliced

3 medium Roma tomatoes, thinly sliced

1/2 teaspoon dried basil

1/2 teaspoon dried oregano

1/4 teaspoon kosher salt

1/4 teaspoon freshly ground black pepper

1 cup shredded fresh mozzarella

In the bottom of a foil pie pan, spread 1/2 cup of the marinara sauce and sprinkle the onion.

Layer the sliced vegetables on top of the marinara in a domino fashion, beginning on the outside and working toward the middle. If some slices are larger than the others, slice them in half for a better fit. Season the layered vegetables with the basil, oregano, salt, and pepper. Drizzle the remaining 1/2 cup marinara sauce over the top.

Stack 4 sheets of heavy-duty aluminum foil large enough to cover and wrap around the pie pan. Bring the longer ends of the foil up into a tent-like shape; fold the foil downward. Seal in the remaining foil ends by curling them inward and under the edges so no fluids escape.

Place the pan flat on top of the hot coals or on a grill grate over the fire. Bake the ratatouille for 30 minutes, then gently remove from the fire and peel the foil back to sprinkle the mozzarella on top. Cover and return the foil pan to the fire. Bake for an additional 10 minutes, until the cheese is melted. Serve immediately.

Apple, Fontina, and Spinach Quesadillas

MAKES 2 QUESADILLAS

Preparation time: 15 minutes

Cooking time: 4 minutes

1 tablespoon Dijon mustard

2 teaspoons apple cider

4 (10-inch) flour tortillas

6 ounces fontina cheese, shredded

1 Fuji apple, cored and cut into $^1/_8$-inch-thick slices

3 cups packed fresh spinach

$^3/_4$ teaspoon freshly ground black pepper

Mix together the Dijon mustard and apple cider in a small bowl. Set aside.

Place 2 iron sandwich makers (or 1 double sandwich maker) inside the fire pit to preheat. Once the irons are heated through, open on a safe surface and spray the inside of the molds with nonstick cooking spray.

Lay 1 flour tortilla inside one of the molds (the tortilla will hang over the sides). Spread a little of the mustard and cider mixture on top of the tortilla inside the mold. Sprinkle the fontina over the mustard spread, then arrange half of the thinly sliced apples on top of the fontina. Lay 1 small handful of spinach leaves on top of the apples, sprinkle with pepper, and then cover with another flour tortilla. Close the iron and trim the edges of the tortilla. Repeat with the other sandwich maker and the remaining ingredients.

Lay the iron sandwich makers flat on top of the hot coals. Allow to cook for roughly 2 minutes per side, rotating frequently until the quesadillas are golden brown. Once the quesadillas are cooked, flip them out onto a plate and allow to cool for 1 minute before serving.

Chicken and Peach Quesadillas with Agave-Lime Sauce

MAKES 4 QUESADILLAS

Preparation time: 20 minutes

Cooking time: 4 minutes

$1/2$ cup low-fat sour cream

1 teaspoon agave nectar

$1^1/2$ tablespoons freshly squeezed lime juice, divided

1 ripe white peach, cubed

2 tablespoons chopped red onion

2 tablespoons chopped red or orange bell pepper

3 tablespoons chopped fresh cilantro

$1/8$ teaspoon sea salt

1 cup cooked chicken breast, shredded into small pieces

8 whole-wheat tortillas

$1/2$ cup shredded pepper Jack cheese

To prepare the sauce, whisk together the sour cream, agave, and 1 tablespoon of the lime juice. Set aside in the refrigerator.

In a medium bowl, combine the peach, onion, bell pepper, cilantro, salt, and the remaining $1/2$ tablespoon lime juice with the chicken. Mix until all ingredients are combined.

Place 4 iron sandwich makers inside the fire pit to preheat. Once the irons are heated through, open on a safe surface and spray the inside of the molds with non-stick cooking spray. Lay 1 whole-wheat tortilla gently inside one of the molds. Place 2 tablespoons of the chicken and peach mixture onto the tortilla, top with $1/4$ cup of the pepper Jack. Lay a second tortilla on top, close the iron, and trim off the excess tortilla. Repeat with the remaining irons and ingredients.

Place the iron sandwich makers flat upon the hot coals. Rotate the irons frequently so that the quesadillas cook evenly on each side, about 2 minutes per side. Once the quesadillas are golden brown, flip them out onto a plate and allow to cool for 1 minute. Serve with the agave-lime sauce.

Spaghetti Iron Sandwich

MAKES 2 SANDWICHES

Preparation time: 10 minutes

Cooking time: 4 to 6 minutes

4 slices Tuscan bread or rustic multigrain bread

2 1/2 cups leftover spaghetti (made with angel hair pasta and marinara or meat sauce)

1/2 cup packed spinach leaves

1/2 cup shredded Havarti cheese or freshly shaved Parmigiano-Reggiano

Sea salt and freshly ground black pepper

Place 2 iron sandwich makers (or 1 double sandwich maker) inside the fire pit to preheat. Once the irons are heated through, open on a safe surface and spray the inside of the molds with nonstick cooking spray. Lay 1 slice of the bread inside one of the molds, and top the bread with about 1 cup of the spaghetti. Place 1/4 cup of the spinach leaves on top of the spaghetti, along with 1/4 cup of the cheese. Season to taste with salt and pepper. Lay another slice of bread on top and gently close the mold, making sure that none of the filling escapes. Repeat with the remaining iron and ingredients.

Lay the iron sandwich makers flat on top of the hot coals. Occasionally rotate the irons, allowing each side to cook for 2 to 3 minutes. The spaghetti sandwich will be a golden-brown color when finished. Flip the sandwiches out of the irons and onto a plate. Serve immediately.

Toss homemade or store-bought vodka sauce with fettuccine noodles for a new take on the traditional spaghetti.

Thanksgiving Sandwich

MAKES 2 SANDWICHES

Preparation time: 5 minutes

Cooking time: 4 to 6 minutes

4 slices cranberry-walnut bread

3 tablespoons cranberry relish

6 slices oven-roasted turkey (12 ounces total)

$^1/_2$ cup shredded muenster cheese

1 cup leftover stuffing

Place 2 iron sandwich makers (or 1 double sandwich maker) inside the fire pit to preheat. Once the irons are heated through, open on a safe surface and spray the inside of the molds with nonstick cooking spray. Lay 1 slice of the bread inside one of the molds. On top of the bread, spread 1$^1/_2$ tablespoons of the cranberry relish and layer 3 slices of the roasted turkey, $^1/_4$ cup of the muenster, and $^1/_2$ cup of the stuffing. Cover with another slice of bread and gently close the iron sandwich maker, making sure the filling does not escape. Repeat with the remaining iron and ingredients.

Lay the iron sandwich makers flat on top of the hot coals. Occasionally rotate the irons so that both sides brown evenly, 2 to 3 minutes per side. Flip the sandwiches out onto a plate and serve immediately.

⊃➞ If you are a fan of Thanksgiving leftovers, add some stuffing to this sandwich for an incredible depth of flavor.

Reuben Sandwich

MAKES 2 SANDWICHES

Preparation time: 10 to 15 minutes

Cooking time: 4 to 6 minutes

RUSSIAN DRESSING

1/4 cup canola mayonnaise

1/4 cup sour cream

1/4 cup ketchup

1 teaspoon Worcestershire sauce

1 tablespoon chili sauce

1/4 cup teaspoon paprika

1/2 teaspoon minced onion

2 teaspoons finely minced dill pickles

SANDWICH

4 slices rye bread

3 ounces corned beef, sliced

1/2 cup sauerkraut, squeezed, drained, and coarsely chopped

1/2 cup shredded Swiss cheese

To make the dressing, combine all of the dressing ingredients together in a bowl and mix well. Cover and set aside in the refrigerator until ready to use.

Place 2 iron sandwich makers (or 1 double sandwich maker) inside the fire pit to preheat. Once the irons are heated through, open on a safe surface and spray the inside of the molds with nonstick cooking spray. Lay 1 slice of the bread inside one of the molds, and spread some of the Russian dressing on top. Arrange 1 1/2 ounces of the corned beef, 1/4 cup of the sauerkraut, and 1/4 cup of the Swiss cheese on top of the dressing. Place a second slice of bread on top and close the mold, making sure no filling escapes. Repeat with the remaining iron and ingredients.

Lay the iron sandwich makers flat inside the fire pit on top of the hot coals. Occasionally rotate the iron sandwich maker so that each side cooks for 2 to 3 minutes, until the bread is a golden-brown color on both sides. Flip the sandwiches out onto a plate and allow to cool for 1 minute before serving.

French Onion Soup Sandwich

MAKES 2 SANDWICHES

Preparation time: 20 minutes

Cooking time: 18 to 20 minutes

1 tablespoon butter

$^1/_2$ tablespoon olive oil

2 yellow onions, sliced

1 teaspoon sea salt

$^1/_2$ teaspoon freshly cracked black pepper

Pinch of sugar

1 teaspoon fresh thyme leaves

3 tablespoons beef broth

4 slices Italian bread

$^1/_2$ cup shredded Gruyère cheese

Melt the butter and olive oil in a saucepot over medium heat. Stir in the onions and sauté for 4 to 5 minutes, until translucent. Add the salt, pepper, sugar and thyme to the onions, and stir until the onions are evenly seasoned. Reduce the heat to low, cover, and allow the onions to cook for 5 minutes, stirring occasionally. When the onions are browned and softened to a mushy consistency, add the beef broth. With a wooden spoon, scrape the bottom of the sauce pot to relieve the extra bits. The liquid will evaporate in about 30 seconds. Remove the pot from the heat, and allow the onions to rest.

Place 2 iron sandwich makers inside (or 1 double sandwich maker) inside the fire pit to preheat. Once the irons are heated through, open on a safe surface and spray the inside of the molds with non-stick cooking spray. Place 1 slice of the bread inside one of the molds. On top of the bread, add 1 heaping tablespoon of the sautéed onions and a good sprinkling of the Gruyère. Cover with another slice of Italian bread and gently close the iron, making sure the filling does not fall out. Repeat with the remaining iron and ingredients.

Lay the iron sandwich makers flat on top of the hot coals for 3 to 4 minutes per side, depending on the temperature of the fire. Occasionally rotate the irons so that the bread toasts evenly to a golden brown color. Flip the sandwiches out onto a plate and serve immediately.

Phyllo-Wrapped Salmon

SERVES 4

Preparation time: 15 minutes

Cooking time: 10 to 12 minutes

4 sheets phyllo dough

1/4 cup plus 2 teaspoons butter, melted, divided

4 pieces skinless salmon fillets

4 tablespoons Dijon mustard

Sea salt and freshly ground black pepper

2 teaspoons freshly squeezed lemon juice

2 teaspoons fresh thyme leaves

Place 1 sheet of phyllo dough on a cutting board, and brush the dough with 1 teaspoon of melted butter. Lay a second sheet of phyllo dough on top. Cut the stacked sheets to make 2 rectangles measuring 7 x 9 inches. Repeat the process with the 2 remaining sheets of phyllo dough and 1 teaspoon of the butter.

Lay 1 salmon fillet on the short side of each phyllo rectangle. Brush each fillet with 1 tablespoon of the Dijon mustard and season with salt and pepper. Roll up the salmon in the dough, and place them seam side down inside a grilling basket. Brush the top of the dough with 1 tablespoon of melted butter before closing the basket. Gently cook the wrapped salmon over the fire pit for 10 to 12 minutes, rotating occasionally so as not to burn the dough. When ready, the phyllo will puff up and turn golden brown, and the salmon will have an opaque color throughout. Remove the wrapped salmon from the fire and allow them to rest for 1 minute before serving. Whisk together the remaining 3 tablespoons melted butter, the lemon juice, and thyme to drizzle on top.

Cedar-Wrapped Cod with Spinach Pesto

SERVES 4

Preparation time: 15 minutes

Cooking time: 8 to 10 minutes

PESTO

1 cup packed spinach leaves

$1/4$ cup grated Parmesan cheese

$1/4$ cup walnuts or pine nuts

1 clove garlic

2 tablespoons lemon zest

2 tablespoons freshly squeezed lemon juice

2 tablespoons lime zest

2 tablespoons freshly squeezed lime juice

$1/4$ cup olive oil

Salt and freshly ground black pepper

FISH

4 (6-ounce) cod fillets

4 sheets cedar paper, soaked according to package directions

Sea salt and freshly ground black pepper

To make the pesto, finely chop the spinach, Parmesan, walnuts, and garlic in a food processor. Add the lemon zest, lemon juice, lime zest, and lime juice to the chopped ingredients. Pulse several times until combined. Set the food processor to a low speed and gradually add the olive oil until well blended. Season to taste with salt and pepper and set aside.

To make the fish, place 1 cod fillet in the center of each individual cedar paper and season with salt and pepper. Fold the long side of the paper edges towards each other and secure with cotton string. Place the wrapped cod fillets inside a grilling basket with the seam side down. Cook over the hot coals for 4 to 5 minutes per side, rotating occasionally so that both sides cook evenly. The cod fillets will look whiter in color and become flaky in texture when cooked through. Gently open the grilling basket, remove the wrapped fillets, and serve on the paper with a dollop of pesto.

⊏⇥ Salmon and halibut are both very tasty alternatives to wrap in cedar.

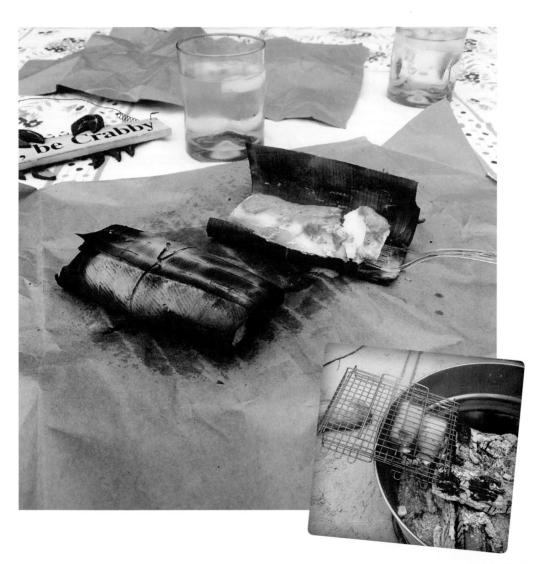

Traditional Calzone

SERVES 4

Preparation time: 10 minutes

Cooking time: 15 to 20 minutes

1 pound pizza dough

$^1/_3$ cup marinara sauce

$^1/_4$ pound pepperoni, thinly sliced

8 ounces mozzarella cheese, shredded

Olive oil, for brushing

Coarse salt

On a lightly floured surface, roll the pizza dough out and into a 10- to 12-inch circle. Spread the marinara sauce on half of the circle, leaving an outside border of a little over 1 inch. Top the marinara sauce with the pepperoni and mozzarella. Fold the plain half of the dough over the dressed half. Beginning on one end, roll and pinch the edges together to seal them. Brush off any excess flour so that it doesn't burn while baking over the fire pit.

Spray the inside of a grilling basket with nonstick cooking spray. Brush the side of the calzone that is facing up with olive oil and sprinkle with salt. Carefully lay the calzone inside the basket, oiled side down. Brush the other side of the calzone with olive oil and sprinkle with salt. Close the basket tightly. Hold the basket over the hot embers in the fire pit, rotating occasionally to prevent burning. Cook the calzone for 8 to 10 minutes per side, depending on how hot the fire is. The calzone is ready when it is golden brown on both sides. Carefully remove the basket from the fire, and allow the calzone to rest for 2 minutes before serving.

≡VARIATIONS≡

There are dozens of filling options for the calzone, and here are some of my favorites: mushrooms, spinach, broccoli, asparagus tips, caramelized onions, chopped bell peppers, artichoke hearts, hot peppers, pineapple, shredded pork, ham, hot or sweet ground sausage, ground beef, chopped chicken, bacon, Swiss cheese, cheddar cheese, goat cheese, Gruyère, blue cheese, Monterey Jack cheese, pepper Jack cheese, and feta cheese.

Iron-Skillet Stuffed Cabbage

SERVES 6

Preparation time: 10 minutes

Cooking time: 15 to 20 minutes

Kosher salt and freshly ground black pepper

1 pound ground beef

1 small onion, chopped

1 cup jasmine rice, uncooked

3 large handfuls cabbage leaves, roughly chopped

1 (8-ounce) can tomato sauce

2 cups chicken stock

1 (14-ounce) can diced tomatoes

1 cup shredded sharp cheddar cheese

Place a large cast-iron skillet on top of the grilling grate over the fire pit. Add the ground beef and onions to the skillet, season with salt and pepper, and cook until the meat has browned. Drain off any grease. Add the rice, cabbage, tomato sauce, chicken stock, and diced tomatoes; stir until combined. Once the mixture comes to a boil, cover with heavy-duty aluminum foil and allow it to simmer for 10 to 15 minutes, until the rice and cabbage become tender and soft. Uncover the skillet, top the mixture with the cheddar, and re-cover so that the cheese can steam and melt. Serve immediately.

> ⤍ For something a little less traditional, substitute kielbasa for the ground beef and add a splash of Worcestershire sauce.

Iron-Skillet Lasagna

SERVES 6

Preparation time: 10 minutes

Cooking time: 10 to 15 minutes

8 ounces lean ground beef

1/4 cup minced onion

1 teaspoon Italian seasoning

Pinch of salt

Pinch of freshly ground black pepper

1 clove garlic, minced

1/2 package oven-ready lasagna noodles, broken into quarters

1 (18- to 24-ounce) can tomato sauce or seasoned pasta sauce

1/4 cup chicken broth

1/2 cup ricotta cheese

1/2 cup shredded mozzarella cheese

Bread, for serving

Place a large cast-iron skillet on top of the grilling grate over the fire pit. Cook the ground beef, onions, Italian seasoning, salt, pepper, and garlic until the meat is cooked through. Add the lasagna noodles, tomato sauce, and chicken broth; stir gently to combine. Bring the mixture to a boil and cook for about 10 to 12 minutes, stirring occasionally to keep the noodles from sticking to the bottom of the skillet. When the noodles are tender, remove the skillet from the fire, and gently stir in the ricotta and mozzarella. Lay 1 sheet of heavy-duty aluminum foil over the top of the skillet and place over the fire again. Once the cheese has melted, remove the skillet from the fire and allow it to cool slightly. Serve with warm bread.

⊏→ For a fresh take on these classic flavors, substitute Alfredo sauce for the tomato sauce, and add 1 cup sliced mushrooms and 2 cups fresh spinach, chopped.

Dutch-Oven Guinness Beef Stew

SERVES 6

Preparation time: 20 minutes

Cooking time: 2 to 3 hours

2 tablespoons all-purpose flour

4 cups beef stock, divided

2 pounds beef stew meat

3 tablespoons vegetable oil

1 tablespoon butter

1 teaspoon kosher salt

1 teaspoon freshly ground black pepper

1 teaspoon cayenne

1 teaspoon sugar

2 onions, roughly chopped

1 clove garlic, chopped

2 tablespoons tomato paste, dissolved in 1 cup water

$1^1/_2$ (11.2-ounce) bottles Guinness

4 whole carrots, unpeeled and roughly sliced

4 new potatoes, quartered

1 sprig thyme

Bread, for serving

In the fire pit, make a large area on one side with the hot embers to place the Dutch-oven on top. Have a small fire burning continuously on the other side of the fire pit.

Mix the flour into 1 cup of the beef stock to dissolve, and pour it into the Dutch oven with all the rest of the ingredients.

Place the lid on top of the Dutch oven, place the oven into the fire pit, and cover the lid with several hot coals. Gradually pile up more hot coals and embers around the Dutch oven as they burn to add more even heat. Cook the stew for 2 to 3 hours, depending on how hot the fire pit and the embers surrounding the Dutch oven are. After 2 hours, carefully check the pot and stir the stew to test the doneness of the vegetables and beef. Once the stew has thickened and the vegetables and beef are tender, remove the pot from the fire pit or move it away from the hot coals. Serve the stew with warm bread.

Mini Macaroni and Cheese Pots

SERVES 4

Preparation time: 15 to 20 minutes

Cooking time: 8 to 10 minutes

2 cups elbow macaroni

1 cup shredded fontina cheese

1/2 cup shredded sharp cheddar cheese

1/2 cup shredded Monterey Jack cheese

4 small terra-cotta pots

2 tablespoons all-purpose flour

1/2 cup milk

3 tablespoons butter

1/2 cup panko breadcrumbs

Prepare the elbow macaroni according to the directions on the package. Set aside.

Mix the fontina, cheddar, and Monterey Jack in a small bowl and set aside. Line the inside of each terra-cotta pot with 1 sheet of heavy-duty aluminum foil and spray with nonstick cooking spray. Evenly distribute 1 cup of macaroni into each pot as the first layer. Evenly distribute 1 cup of the cheese mixture among the pots and top with the remaining pasta. Cover the last layer of pasta with the remaining 1 cup of the cheese mixture. Mix the flour and milk to make a slurry, and pour it evenly into the pots. Top each macaroni pot with the melted butter and panko breadcrumbs.

Stack 4 sheets of heavy-duty aluminum foil for each pot. Place each pot in the center of a foil stack and create a tent-like shape over the pot. Wrap the opposite sides inward, and seal the edges tight so that no liquid escapes.

In the fire pit, make a large area on one side with the coals to place the pots, leaving the other side to burn a small fire. Place the pots inside the fire pit, and pack the hot coals around the pots, leaving room in between for even baking. Bake the pots for 8 to 10 minutes, depending on how hot the coals are, and occasionally rotate the pots with tongs. To check for doneness, remove a macaroni pot from the fire and carefully unwrap it. The macaroni should be crispy on the edges and the cheese melted. Remove immediately from the fire pit once they have cooked properly. Allow to cool for 5 minutes before serving. The pots will be hot.

Bruschetta Pizza

MAKES 4 SERVINGS

Preparation time: 5 minutes

Cooking time: 10 to 12 minutes

1 clove garlic, minced

2 tablespoons olive oil

1 (13.8-ounce) can refrigerated pizza dough

$^1/_4$-$^1/_2$ cup canned roasted tomatoes (in olive oil), chopped

$^1/_2$ cup packed spinach leaves

$^1/_2$ cup kalamata olives, sliced

1 cup freshly crumbled mozzarella cheese

In a small bowl, mix together the garlic and olive oil. Set aside.

Place a grill grate over the fire pit. Unroll the pizza dough onto a flat grill tray sprayed with oil, and place the tray onto the grill grate Allow the dough to cook on the bottom until slightly brown, roughly 5 to 6 minutes, and then flip over with a steel spatula. Immediately remove the pizza from the fire, and then brush the olive oil and garlic mixture on just the edges of the pizza dough. Inside the edges of the dough, spread out the tomatoes with a bit of the flavored oil. Top with the spinach, olives, and mozzarella. Place the pizza back on the fire for 5 to 6 minutes, until the cheese has melted and the bottom of the dough is a light golden brown. Remove the grill tray from the fire pit, cut the pizza into slices, and serve immediately.

Rustic White Pizza with Scallops and Pancetta

SERVES 4

Preparation time: 10 to 12 minutes

Cooking time: 10 to 12 minutes

1 tablespoon butter

1 cup sea scallops, thinly sliced

Pinch of salt

Pinch of freshly ground black pepper

$1/2$ cup chopped pancetta (½-inch pieces

1 (13.8-ounce) can refrigerated pizza dough

3 tablespoons olive oil

1 clove garlic, minced

$1/2$ cup cherry tomatoes, halved

$3/4$ cup shredded Parmigiano-Reggiano cheese

In a small pan, melt the butter and sauté the scallops until tender. Season with salt and pepper, remove from the pan, and set aside. Add the pancetta to the pan and sauté until slightly crispy. Remove the pancetta from the pan and set aside. Mix the olive oil and garlic in a small bowl and set aside.

Place a grill grate over the fire pit. Unroll the pizza dough onto a flat grill tray sprayed with oil, and place the tray onto the grill grate. Allow the dough to cook on the bottom until slightly brown, roughly 5 to 6 minutes, and then flip over with a steel spatula. Immediately remove the dough from the fire and brush the olive oil and garlic mixture on top. Evenly cover the dough with the scallops, pancetta, tomatoes, and Parmigiano-Reggiano.

Place the pizza back on the fire for 5 to 6 minutes, until the cheese has melted and the bottom of the dough is a light golden brown. Remove the grill tray from the fire pit, cut the pizza into slices, and serve immediately.

≡VARIATIONS≡

SEAFOOD PIZZA: Add $1/2$ cup chopped cooked shrimp and a few dashes of Old Bay seasoning to the scallop pizza.

PULLED PORK PIZZA: Top the grilled pizza dough with 1 cup leftover BBQ pulled pork, $1/4$ cup blue cheese, $3/4$ cup mozzarella cheese, and a small handful of spinach leaves.

Grilled Stuffed Flank Steak

SERVES 4 TO 6

Preparation time: 20 to 25 minutes

Cooking time: 11 to 16 minutes

2 cloves garlic, minced

4 scallions, thinly sliced

1/4 cup chopped fresh flat-leaf parsley

1/2 cup chopped fresh mushrooms

8 ounces fontina cheese, shredded

1/2 cup freshly grated Parmigiano-Reggiano cheese

1/2 cup panko breadcrumbs

1/4 cup olive oil

1 (2- to 2 1/2-pound) whole flank steak, trimmed of fat

Kosher salt and freshly ground black pepper

In a medium bowl, combine the garlic, scallions, parsley, mushrooms, fontina, Parmigiano-Reggiano, and breadcrumbs; mix well. Add the olive oil and mix again. Set aside.

On a cutting board, lay out the steak and trim the long edges to create a clean rectangle. Holding the steak flat, carefully butterfly the steak with a sharp boning knife. Leave the back edge attached by 1/4 to 1/2 inch of meat. Open the steak and flatten the seam gently with your hand to form a large flat rectangle.

Season the steak on the exposed sides with salt and pepper. Spread the stuffing mixture evenly over the beef, leaving a 1/2-inch border along the side farthest from you. Press and gently pack the stuffing mixture onto the beef to keep it in place. Starting from the side nearest you, roll up the meat in jelly-roll fashion, making sure to press in any stuffing that falls out of the ends of the steak roll.

Tie the beef tightly with pieces of cooking twine, spacing the ties evenly every 1 1/2 inches. Insert a skewer through each piece of twine and push through to the other side of the rolled-up steak. Using a sharp knife, cut carefully between the ties to make individual pinwheels. Season each one with salt and pepper.

Place a grilling grate over the fire pit, then clean it and spray it with nonstick cooking spray. (You can also use a grilling basket, but be sure to spray the inside and outside with

nonstick cooking spray.) Place the steak pinwheels on the hottest side of the fire pit and cook, without moving, until charred on the first side, 3 to 4 minutes. Flip the steaks and continue the grilling process on the cooler side of the fire pit until a thermometer inserted in the center reads between 120°F (medium-rare) and 130°F (medium), 8 to 12 minutes. Once the steak has reached the proper temperature, remove the pinwheels from the grill, cover, and allow to rest for 5 minutes before serving.

At Sunset

Sugar Mama Pie

MAKES 2 SANDWICH PIES

Preparation time: 7 minutes

Cooking time: 4 to 8 minutes

1 tablespoon brown sugar

1 tablespoon butter, melted

1 1/2 teaspoons light corn syrup

2 whole bananas, halved lengthwise and cut into thirds

4 slices multigrain bread

2 1/2 tablespoons creamy peanut butter

2 1/2 tablespoons peach or strawberry preserves

To make the caramel glaze for the bananas, mix the brown sugar, melted butter, and light corn syrup in a small bowl. Toss the bananas in the mixture, coating well.

Place 2 iron sandwich makers (or 1 double sandwich maker) inside the fire pit to preheat. Once the irons are heated through, open on a safe surface and spray the inside of the molds with nonstick cooking spray. Lay 3 banana slices inside each iron and close. Gently rotate the bananas over the hot fire pit until they turn golden brown, roughly 2 to 4 minutes. Remove the bananas from the hot irons and set aside.

To build the sugar mama,* spray the inside of the iron sandwich makers with nonstick cooking spray. Lay 1 slice of bread inside each side of both irons. Spread 1 heaping tablespoon of peanut butter on 1 slice of the bread and 1 heaping tablespoon of the preserves on the other slice. Lay the caramelized bananas on top of the peanut butter and carefully close the mold. Place the hot iron sandwich makers back inside the fire pit, flat on top of the hot embers. Occasionally rotate the irons so that each side cooks for 2 to 4 minutes. When the bread is golden brown on both sides, remove the irons from the fire, flip the sandwiches out onto a plate, and allow to cool for 1 minute before serving. Enjoy!

---

*The Sugar Mama Pie is a delicious dessert created by my dad.

Blueberry, Marshmallow, and Chocolate Pie

MAKES 2 SANDWICH PIES

Preparation time: 5 minutes

Cooking time: 4 to 6 minutes

4 slices multigrain bread or whole-wheat bread

2 thin slices Havarti cheese

1/2 cup frozen blueberries, thawed

2-3 tablespoons mini chocolate chips

1/2 cup mini marshmallows

Place 2 iron sandwich makers (or 1 double sandwich maker) inside the fire pit to preheat. Once the irons are heated through, open on a safe surface and spray the inside of the molds with the butter-favored nonstick cooking spray. Lay 1 slice of bread inside one of the molds. On top of the bread, lay a slice of Havarti cheese, ¼ cup of the blueberries, 1 to 1½ tablespoons of the mini chocolate chips, and ¼ cup of the mini marshmallows. Cover with a second slice of bread and gently close the sandwich maker. Repeat with the remaining iron and ingredients.

Lay the iron sandwich makers flat on top of the hot coals. Occasionally rotate the irons so that both sides brown evenly, 2 to 3 minutes per side. Occasionally check the sandwich so that it does not burn. When the bread is golden brown, remove the irons from the fire, flip the blueberry sandwiches out onto a plate, and allow to cool for 1 minute before serving.

Chocolate-Raspberry Pound-Cake Pie

MAKES 2 SANDWICH PIES

Preparation time: 5 minutes

Cooking time: 4 to 6 minutes

4 thick slices pound cake

4 tablespoons mascarpone cheese, softened

1/2 cup frozen raspberries, thawed (if using fresh raspberries, add 1/2 teaspoon sugar to them and allow to sit)

1 (1.55-ounce) bar Hershey's milk chocolate, broken into sections

Zest of 1 orange

Place 2 iron sandwich makers (or 1 double sandwich maker) inside the fire pit to preheat. Once the irons are heated through, open on a safe surface and spray the inside of the molds with butter-favored nonstick cooking spray. Gently lay 1 slice of the pound cake inside one of the molds and spread with 2 tablespoons of the mascarpone. On top of the mascarpone, layer 1/4 cup of the raspberries, half of the chocolate pieces, and a sprinkling of orange zest. Cover with a second slice of pound cake and gently close the iron. Repeat with the remaining iron and ingredients.

Lay the iron sandwich makers flat on top of the hot coals. Occasionally rotate the irons so that both sides brown evenly, 2 to 3 minutes per side. When the pound cake is golden brown, remove the irons from the fire, flip the sandwiches out onto a plate, and allow to cool for 1 minute before serving.

Roasted Strawberry, Brie, and Chocolate Pie

MAKES 2 SANDWICH PIES

Preparation time: 5 minutes

Cooking time: 4 to 6 minutes

4 slices multigrain bread, thickly sliced

5 strawberries, thinly sliced

2-3 ounces brie cheese, sliced and rind removed

2-4 tablespoons mini chocolate chips

1/4 teaspoon salt

Place 2 iron sandwich makers (or 1 double sandwich maker) inside the fire pit to preheat. Once the irons are heated through, open on a safe surface and spray the inside of the molds with butter-favored nonstick cooking spray. Lay 1 slice of the bread inside one of the molds and arrange half of the strawberries on top. Top the strawberries with half of the brie and 2 tablespoons of the mini chocolate chips, sprinkling with a pinch of salt. Cover with a second slice of bread and gently close the iron. Repeat with the remaining iron and ingredients.

Lay the iron sandwich makers flat on top of the hot coals. Occasionally rotate the irons so that both sides brown evenly, 2 to 3 minutes per side. When the bread is golden brown, remove the irons from the fire, flip the sandwiches out onto a plate, and allow to cool for 1 minute before serving.

Rice Krispies Treat S'mores

SERVES 8

Preparation time: 2 to 3 minutes, plus 45 minutes to prepare the treats

Cooking time: 8 minutes to 10 minutes

RICE KRISPIES TREATS

Recipe adapted from Kellogg's

3 tablespoons butter

4 cups mini marshmallows

6 cups Rice Krispies cereal

S'MORES

6-8 ounces mini chocolate chips

8 extra-large square marshmallows

To make the Rice Krispies treats, combine the butter and mini marshmallows in a saucepot over medium heat. Stir constantly until the marshmallows are melted. Pour the cereal into the saucepan and stir until coated.

Grease a 12 x 17-inch cookie sheet with nonstick cooking spray, and spoon the cereal mixture into the pan. Using a spatula sprayed with nonstick spray, spread the mixture evenly in the pan. Cover with plastic wrap and gently press down any uneven areas. The mixture will harden in 30 to 40 minutes. Once the mixture is firm, use a large round cookie cutter or cup to cut at least 8 individual circles out of the sheet. Place the treats in a ziplock bag and store in a dry place until ready to use.

To make the s'mores, place the chocolate chips in a micro-wave-safe bowl and heat in the microwave in 30-second increments until the chocolate is melted through. The chocolate chips can also be heated over the fire pit in a small steal camping pot until melted through.

Skewer the marshmallows onto roasting forks and toast to your liking. Once the marshmallows are toasted, place them on top of round Rice Krispies treats and top with a second treat. Dip the s'more sandwiches into the melted chocolate and enjoy.

Bite-Size Strawberry Angel Food Cake with Chocolate

SERVES 8

Preparation time: 5 minutes

Cooking time: 2 to 3 minutes

8 cubes angel food cake, cut into 1-1½-inch cubes

8 large strawberries, stemmed

¼ cup chocolate topping, warmed

Skewer the angel food cake and strawberries onto roasting forks. Occasionally rotate the forks over the fire pit until the cake turns golden brown and the strawberries soften, 2 to 3 minutes. Remove from the fire pit and serve immediately with the warm chocolate topping.

Cookie S'mores with Hershey's Chocolate

SERVES 4

Preparation time: 1 minute

Cooking time: 1 to 2 minutes

8 large marshmallows

8 large cut-out sugar cookies or other favorite cookies

1 (1.55-ounce) bar Hershey's milk chocolate, broken into sections

Skewer the marshmallows onto roasting forks, making sure both prongs go through the marshmallow for better stability. Occasionally rotate the marshmallows over the fire pit for 1 to 2 minutes, until they turn golden brown on the outside and gooey on the inside. Remove the forks from the fire pit. Stack a few pieces of the Hershey's bar onto the top of 4 upside-down cookies. With the marshmallows still on the fork, place them on top of the chocolate, and then top with a second cookie right side up. Press the cookies together while slowly removing the forks from the marshmallows. The cookie s'mores will be gooey and warm.

≡VARIATION≡

BROWNIE S'MORES: Replace the cookies with 4 thick-cut brownies sliced in half horizontally.

Cinnamon-Sugar Twists with Mascarpone Funfetti Dip

MAKES 8 TWISTS

Preparation time: 20 minutes

Cooking time: 5 to 8 minutes

DIP

¹/₂ of a (15.25-ounce) box Funfetti cake mix

8 ounces mascarpone cheese

6 tablespoons milk

¹/₂ teaspoon vanilla extract

TWISTS

¹/₈ cup sugar

¹/₂ tablespoon ground cinnamon

1 sheet puff pastry, thawed

2 tablespoons butter, melted

Presoak the dowel rods in water for roughly 45 minutes to 1 hour prior to cooking. For longer use, it is best to soak the dowel rods overnight. To make the dip, use a hand-held mixer or standing mixer to cream the Funfetti cake mix with the mascarpone cheese until the batter is thick and smooth. Slowly add in the milk and vanilla until the batter becomes creamy and fluffy. Cover and place in the refrigerator until ready to use.

To make the sticks, mix the sugar and cinnamon in a small bowl. Set aside. On a lightly floured sheet of parchment paper, unwrap the puff pastry and sprinkle with flour. Roll the pastry into a 10 x 10-inch square. Brush both sides of the pastry sheet with the butter and sprinkle with the cinnamon-sugar mixture. Use a pizza cutter to cut the sheet into 2-inch strips, roughly 8 strips total.

Spray the presoaked wooden dowels or sweet sticks with nonstick cooking spray. Twist the puff pastry around sweet sticks (see page 10). The trick is to slightly overlap the pastry as it is twisted around the stick. To seal the end, tuck the final 2 inches under the previous overlap. Gently hold the sticks over the hot flames for 5 to 8 minutes, until the twists puff up and turn golden brown. Be sure to occasionally rotate the sticks so that the pastry browns evenly and does not burn. Serve warm with the Funfetti dip.

⟤VARIATIONS⟥

FRUIT TWISTS: Instead of cinnamon and sugar, spread ¼ cup of your favorite fruit preserves over the puff pastry before twisting. Dust the cooked twists with powdered sugar and enjoy as breakfast or dessert.

Try these other dips that pair deliciously with the Cinnamon-Sugar Twists:

CREAMY PUMPKIN DIP: Mix together 8 ounces cream cheese, softened; ¾ cup powdered sugar; 1 cup pumpkin puree; 1 tablespoon pumpkin pie spice; and 8 ounces Cool Whip until creamy, for a new fall favorite.

DARK CHOCOLATE DIP: Cream together 8 ounces cream cheese, softened; ⅓ cup vanilla Greek yogurt; 4 ounces dark chocolate, melted; 1 cup powdered sugar; 2 teaspoons vanilla extract; and 8 ounces Cool Whip.

Crispy Wonton Cups with Lemon Mousse

SERVES 8

Preparation time: 15 minutes

Cooking time: 5 to 6 minutes

LEMON MOUSSE

1 1/2 cups heavy cream

8 ounces light cream cheese, softened

1/2 cup sugar

1/4 cup freshly squeezed lemon juice

1 tablespoon lemon zest

1 pint raspberries

WONTON CUPS

8 circular wonton wrappers

To make the lemon mousse, whip the heavy cream with a hand-held mixer or stand mixer on medium-high speed until semi-firm peaks form, roughly 1 minute. In a separate bowl, mix the softened cream cheese, sugar, lemon juice, and lemon zest. Gently fold the whipped cream into the cream cheese mixture until well combined. Chill the mousse in the refrigerator until ready to use.

Use nonstick cooking spray to lightly mist the outside of the cup on the Tarts on Fire tool. Fold the wonton wrapper around the cup and press tightly. Gently hold the tool over the hot fire pit coals and rotate slowly. The wonton will begin to puff up and turn golden brown. Once the entire wonton cup has puffed up, carefully remove the tool from the fire, and flip the wonton onto a plate to cool. Once the wontons have cooled, fill them with the lemon mousse and top with the fresh raspberries. Serve and enjoy!

> ⇒ Fill the wonton cups with Italian ice or your favorite frozen yogurt. Yummy!

Flame-Crisped Cannoli

MAKES 6 CANNOLI

Preparation time: 15 minutes

Cooking time: 10 minutes

1/2 cup mascarpone cheese, softened

2 tablespoons cup ricotta cheese

Zest of 1/2 orange

6 tablespoons confectioner's sugar, plus more for dusting

1/4 cup heavy cream, whipped

1 (8-ounce) can refrigerated crescent dough

1/4 cup mini chocolate chips

⌦ Fill the cannoli with vanilla cream and top with melted chocolate to enjoy a fire-pit éclair. Jumbo biscuit dough is a good alternative to the crescent dough.

To make the filling, thoroughly mix the mascarpone, ricotta, and orange zest in a bowl. Add the 6 tablespoons confectioner's sugar and whisk until smooth. Do not overmix. Fold the whipped cream into the mixture until combined. Cover the filling and refrigerate for at least 1 hour. It can also be made 1 day in advance and refrigerated overnight.

To make the cannoli shells, unroll the crescent dough and cut it into 6 even squares. Lightly mist a sweet stick or presoaked wooden dowel (see page 10) with nonstick cooking spray. Gently wrap 1 dough square around the stick in a diamond shape, overlapping two of the corners and sealing them together. The two opposite corners will stick out. Carefully hold the stick over the hot coals and flames. Cook the cannoli shell until puffed up and golden brown, 8 to 10 minutes. Occasionally rotate the stick so that the cannoli shell browns evenly and does not burn. Repeat with the rest of the dough squares.

Allow the shells to cool before filling with the cannoli cream. While the shells cool, spoon the filling into a pastry bag. (You can also use a ziplock bag with one lower corner snipped to squeeze out the filling.) Place the tip of the bag into one end of a cooled shell and gently squeeze enough filling to reach the center. Repeat the process on the other end of the shell. Once all the shells are filled, gently dip the cream-filled ends into the mini chocolate chips. Dust with the remaining confectioner's sugar and enjoy!

Cappuccino Cream-Filled Phyllo Cups

SERVES 6

Preparation time: 15 minutes

1 tablespoon instant espresso powder

1 cup whipping cream, chilled

2 tablespoons sweetened condensed milk

1/4 teaspoon ground cinnamon

Pinch of coarse salt

12 phyllo cups (recipe follows)

1/2 teaspoon unsweetened cocoa powder

In a mixing bowl, combine the espresso powder with a small amount of the whipping cream and stir until the powder dissolves. Add the remaining whipping cream, condensed milk, cinnamon, and salt. Whisk all the ingredients until firm, but do not allow dry peaks to form. Refrigerate the cappuccino cream until ready to fill the phyllo cups.

Fill the phyllo cups with the cappuccino cream and top with a sprinkling of the cocoa powder. Serve immediately.

PHYLLO CUPS

MAKES 12 CUPS

Preparation time: 12 minutes

Cooking time: 4 to 6 minutes per cup

6 (13 x 17-inch) phyllo sheets

6 tablespoons (3/4 stick) unsalted butter, melted

6 tablespoons (3/4 stick) unsalted butter, melted

Lay 1 sheet of phyllo on a large cutting board. (Keep the remaining phyllo under a damp towel.) Brush the entire top of the sheet with melted butter. Lay another sheet of phyllo on top of the first and repeat until all 6 layers have been stacked and brushed with butter.

Using a sharp knife, cut the phyllo dough into 12 squares measuring 4 by 4 inches. Wrap and mold 1 dough square around the cup of the Tarts on Fire tool. Place the tool over the hot fire for 4 to 6 minutes, until the cup is toasted and golden brown. Occasionally rotate the tool so that the phyllo cup cooks evenly. Remove the phyllo cup from the tool and set aside to cool. Repeat the process with the remaining 11 dough squares.

Pumpkin Pie Cups

SERVES 6

Preparation time: 40 minutes

1 (3.4-ounce) package instant vanilla pudding mix

$^1/_2$ cup cold milk

$^1/_2$ cup canned pumpkin puree

$^1/_2$ teaspoon ground cinnamon

$^1/_4$ teaspoon ground nutmeg

4 ounces Cool Whip topping, thawed

3 tablespoons caramel sauce topping

3 chopped tablespoons pecans

12 phyllo cups (page 111)

In a mixing bowl, whisk the pudding mix, milk, pumpkin, cinnamon, and nutmeg. Fold in $^3/_4$ cup of the Cool Whip until well combined. Cover the bowl with plastic wrap and place in the refrigerator for 25 to 30 minutes, until chilled and slightly thickened.

Pour $^1/_2$ teaspoon of the caramel topping into the bottom of each phyllo cup, then top with $^1/_2$ teaspoon of the pecans. Distribute the pumpkin filling into the phyllo cups and top with the remaining Cool Whip, caramel sauce, and pecans.

> ⊃➙ This pumpkin filling is also delicious inside flaky buttermilk biscuit cups (see the recipe for Key Lime Pie Cups on page 113).

Key Lime Pie Cups

SERVES 8

Preparation time: 30 to 35 minutes

Cooking time: 3 to 5 minutes per cup

1 (14-ounce) can sweetened condensed milk

1 teaspoon finely shredded key lime peel or lime peel

¹/₂ cup key lime juice or freshly squeezed lime juice

2 cups whipping cream

1 (16.3-ounce) can jumbo buttermilk biscuits

Graham cracker crumbs, for topping

Mix the sweetened condensed milk, lime peel, and lime juice in a mixing bowl. In another mixing bowl, beat the cream with a hand-held mixer or stand mixer on medium speed until soft peaks form. Fold half of the whipped cream into the lime mixture until well combined. Cover the bowl with plastic wrap and place in the refrigerator for 25 to 30 minutes, until chilled and slightly set. Cover and refrigerate the remaining whipped cream.

In the meantime, mold 1 biscuit over the Tarts on Fire tool. Bake the biscuit over the hot coals in the fire pit for 3 to 5 minutes, until golden brown. Occasionally rotate the tart tool so that the biscuit bakes evenly and does not burn. Remove the tool from the fire and transfer the biscuit onto a plate to cool. Repeat the process for the remaining 7 biscuits.

When the key lime filling is slightly set and the biscuits have cooled, evenly distribute the filling among the cups and top with the remaining whipped cream and crushed graham crackers.

Mini Brownie Pots

4 small terra-cotta pots

$3/4$ cup cocoa powder

$1/2$ teaspoon baking soda

$2/3$ cup butter, melted, divided

$1/2$ cup water, boiling

1 cup granulated sugar

1 cup firmly packed light brown sugar

2 eggs

$1 1/3$ cup all-purpose flour

1 teaspoon vanilla extract

$1/4$ teaspoon salt

1 cup chocolate chips

Vanilla ice cream or whipped cream, for serving

Line each terra-cotta pot with 1 sheet of heavy-duty aluminum foil, and then spray the inside with nonstick cooking spray. Set aside.

In a large bowl, combine the cocoa powder and baking soda, add $1/3$ cup of the butter, and mix to combine. Add the boiling water and stir until the mixture thickens. Add the granulated and brown sugars, eggs, and the remaining $1/3$ cup melted butter; mix thoroughly. Stir in the flour, vanilla, and salt; blend until smooth. Stir in the chocolate chips until combined. Pour the batter evenly into each pot.

Stack 3 sheets of heavy-duty aluminum foil for each pot, and place 1 pot into the center of each stack. Fold the opposite sides of the foil upwards to create a tent-like shape, then fold downward and curl the sides inward to seal the packets tight so that no brownie batter leaks out.

Place the wrapped pots in between the hot coals, spacing them evenly apart to ensure even baking. Bake the brownie pots for 10 to 12 minutes, depending on how hot the fire pit is. To check for doneness, use tongs to remove one of the pots from the fire, and then carefully unfold the foil. The brownie will have a cake-like center and firm sides when ready. Carefully remove the other brownie pots and allow to cool for 5 to 10 minutes before serving. Enjoy with vanilla ice cream or whipped cream.

Mini Chocolate-Chip Monkey Breads

SERVES 6

Preparation time: 15 minutes

Cooking time: 10 to 12 minutes

6 small terra-cotta pots

2 (16.3-ounce) cans jumbo buttermilk biscuits

1/3 cup granulated sugar

Pinch of coarse salt

1/2 cup (1 stick) unsalted butter, melted

3/4 cup firmly packed light brown sugar

1/2 cup mini chocolate chips

Line each terra-cotta pot with 1 sheet of parchment paper, and then spray the inside with non-stick cooking spray.

Open both cans of biscuits, and cut each biscuit into 6 pieces. Place the sugar, salt, and biscuit pieces in a ziplock bag. Seal the bag and shake until each piece is well coated. In a small bowl, mix the melted butter with the brown sugar. Set aside. Fill each pot halfway with the biscuit pieces. Sprinkle 2 teaspoons of chocolate chips inside each pot. Distribute the remaining biscuit pieces inside each pot and sprinkle with another 2 teaspoons of chocolate chips per pot. Pour the melted butter and brown sugar mixture evenly over the top of the dough in each pot.

Stack 3 sheets of heavy-duty aluminum foil for each pot, and place 1 pot in the center of each stack. Fold the opposite sides of the foil upwards to create a tent-like shape. Seal the top and sides shut so that no juices spill out while baking.

To bake the pots properly, create a flat area in the fire pit with red-hot embers on one side and a small fire on the other. Bury the pots in the hot embers so that each pot is surrounded by the coals. Be sure to leave enough space between pots for the embers to burn and provide even baking. Occasionally rotate the pots using large fire tongs. The individual monkey breads should bake for 8 to 10 minutes, until the tops are light brown and the sides golden brown. Depending on how hot the embers are, the baking time may be longer. Remove the pots from the fire, and immediately flip them over onto a flat surface or plate to stop the cooking process. Peel the parchment paper off the bread and serve warm.

≡ VARIATION ≡

CHOCOLATE CHOCOLATE-CHIP MONKEY BREAD: Add 3 tablespoons unsweetened cocoa powder to the brown sugar and butter mixture.

Mini Caramel-Pecan Monkey Breads

SERVES 6

Preparation time: 20 minutes

Cooking time: 10 to 12 minutes

6 small terra-cotta pots

2/3 cup granulated sugar

1 tablespoon ground cinnamon

Pinch of coarse salt

2 (16.3-ounce) cans jumbo buttermilk biscuits

1 cup pecan pieces, toasted

3/4 cup (1 1/2 sticks) butter

1 cup firmly packed light brown sugar

1/3 cup French vanilla coffee creamer

2 teaspoons vanilla extract

Line each terra-cotta pot with 1 sheet of parchment paper, and then spray the inside with nonstick cooking spray.

Mix the granulated sugar, cinnamon, and coarse salt in a ziplock bag. Set aside.

Open both cans of biscuits, and cut each biscuit into 6 pieces. Add the biscuit pieces to the cinnamon-sugar mixture. Seal the bag and shake until each piece is well coated.

Sprinkle 1 tablespoon of the pecans into the bottom of each pot. Layer 1/3 cup of the coated biscuit pieces on top of the pecans. Sprinkle another 1 tablespoon of pecans into each pot and arrange the remaining biscuit pieces on top. Sprinkle any remaining cinnamon sugar over each pot. Top with the remaining toasted pecans, distributing evenly.

Heat the butter, brown sugar, and coffee creamer in a small saucepot over low or in the microwave. When the butter is melted, stir in the vanilla extract. Pour the caramel sauce gently and evenly over the top of the dough in each pot.

Stack 3 sheets of heavy-duty aluminum foil for each pot, and place 1 pot in the center of each stack. Fold the opposite sides of the foil upwards to create a tent-like shape. Seal the top and sides shut so that no juices spill out while baking.

To bake the pots properly, create a flat area in the fire pit with red-hot embers on one side and a small fire on the other. Bury the pots in the hot embers so that each pot is surrounded by the coals. Be sure to leave enough space between pots for the embers to burn and provide even baking. Occasionally rotate the pots using large fire tongs. The individual monkey breads should bake for 8 to 10 minutes, until the tops are light brown and the sides golden brown. Depending on how hot the embers are, the baking time may be longer. Remove the pots from the fire, and immediately flip them over onto a flat surface or plate to stop the cooking process. Peel the parchment paper off the bread and serve warm.

Peach and Raspberry Cobbler

SERVES 6

Preparation time: 15 minutes

Cooking time: 13 to 18 minutes

FILLING

4 cups peeled and sliced fresh peaches

2 cups fresh raspberries

$1/4$ cup water

2 tablespoons sugar substitute

4 teaspoons cornstarch

1 tablespoon freshly squeezed lemon juice

$1/4$ teaspoon ground allspice

BISCUIT TOPPING

1 cup all-purpose flour

2 tablespoons sugar substitute

$3/4$ teaspoon baking powder

$1/4$ teaspoon baking soda

$1/4$ teaspoon allspice

$1/8$ teaspoon salt

$1/3$ cup low-fat yogurt

$1/4$ cup eggs (or 1 egg, beaten)

2 tablespoons butter, melted

Spray the inside of a 9-inch foil pan with nonstick cooking spray.

To make the filling, combine the peaches, raspberries, water, sugar substitute, cornstarch, lemon juice, and allspice in a medium bowl. Pour the filling into the foil pan and set aside.

Thoroughly combine all of the biscuit ingredients in a mixing bowl; the batter will be sticky in texture. Dollop the batter on top of the filling by spoonfuls until all the biscuit batter is used.

Stack 4 large sheets of heavy-duty aluminum foil, and place the foil pan in the center. Cover the pan with a second foil pan to make a dome. Wrap the foil around both pans to seal the juices inside. Carefully place the cobbler inside the fire pit on top of the hot coals or on a grilling grate. The cobbler should bake on one side for 8 to 10 minutes. Use tongs or fire gloves to flip the cobbler over. Allow it to cook for an additional 6 to 8 minutes, depending on how hot the fire is. The biscuits will be golden brown when ready to remove from the fire. Allow to cool for 5 minutes before serving.

> ☞ If you have an extra can of biscuits on hand, you can use them to top the filling instead of mixing your own batter.

Cast-Iron Bananas Foster

SERVES 2 TO 4

Preparation time: 2 minutes

Cooking time: 4 to 6 minutes

4 ripe bananas, cut into 1-inch-thick slices

1/3 cup firmly packed light brown sugar

1/4 cup butter

2 tablespoons rum

Vanilla ice cream, for serving

In a cast-iron skillet on the grilling grate, combine the bananas, brown sugar, and butter. Toss the banana mixture occasionally until caramelized, 3 to 5 minutes depending on how hot the fire is. Add the rum and allow the bananas to cook for about 1 minute. Pour the caramelized bananas over a scoop of vanilla ice cream in a serving bowl. Serve immediately and enjoy.

Cast-Iron Apple Crisp

SERVES 6

Preparation time: 20 minutes

Cooking time: 15 to 18 minutes

$^1/_4$ cup flour

$^3/_4$ cup quick oats

$^3/_4$ cup firmly packed brown sugar

1 stick unsalted butter, cut into small cubes

1 teaspoon ground cinnamon

1 tablespoon granulated sugar

6-8 tart apples (such as McIntosh or Granny Smith)

$^1/_2$ cup water

Vanilla ice cream or whipped cream, for serving

In a mixing bowl, combine the flour, quick oats, and brown sugar. Using your hands, work the butter into the oat mixture to create a coarse texture. Set aside. Combine the cinnamon and granulated sugar in a small bowl. Set aside.

Peel and core the apples, then cut them into $^1/_4$- to $^1/_2$-inch-thick slices. Place the slices in a large cast-iron skillet and toss with the cinnamon-sugar until coated. Carefully pour the water into the bottom of the skillet. Top the apples with the oat mixture, distributing evenly. Do not press the topping in between the apples.

Place the skillet on a grilling grate or flat on top of the hot embers. Allow the apple crisp to cook for 10 to 15 minutes, until the apples become soft and the topping has begun to brown. The baking time will vary depending on the heat of the fire. Remove the skillet from the fire and allow to cool. The apple crisp will continue to cook as it sits. Serve with vanilla ice cream or whipped cream.

Dutch-Oven Oreo-Chocolate Cake

SERVES 6 TO 8

Preparation time: 12 minutes

Cooking time: 20 to 30 minutes

1 (15- to 16-ounce) box devil's food cake mix

$^3/_4$ cup (1$^1/_2$ sticks) salted butter, melted

$^2/_3$ cup evaporated milk, divided

1 (14.3-ounce) package Oreo cookies, crushed

1 (12-ounce) bag chocolate chunks

Kosher salt

Vanilla ice cream, for serving

Line a 10-inch Dutch oven with heavy-duty aluminum foil. Place the pot on top of the hot coals to preheat.

In a large bowl, mix the cake mix, melted butter, and $^1/_3$ cup of the evaporated milk. Remove the lid from the hot Dutch oven, spread half of the cake mixture in the bottom of the pot, and replace the lid. Arrange several hot coals on top of the lid, and allow the cake to bake for roughly 6 minutes.

While the bottom layer cooks, place three-quarters of the crushed Oreo cookies in a bowl with the remaining $^1/_3$ cup evaporated milk; mix well. Remove the lid from the Dutch oven, pour the Oreo mixture on top of the cake, and sprinkle the mixture with the chocolate chunks. Arrange dollops of the remaining cake batter over the top. Do not spread the batter. Sprinkle lightly with kosher salt, and then replace the lid. Cook for an additional 15 to 20 minutes, depending on how hot the coals are. The cake should have a fudge-like consistency on top but be more firm on the bottom. To remove the cake, carefully lift the foil from the pot and place on a plate. Serve warm with vanilla ice cream.

About the Author

Vanessa Bante is a baking and pastry chef with a strong culinary background. In her travels across the United States, she has learned about different styles of food and enjoys creating new deconstructed recipes from what she has tasted along the way. She and her family are avid fire pit users. In her spare time, she writes short stories.

Index

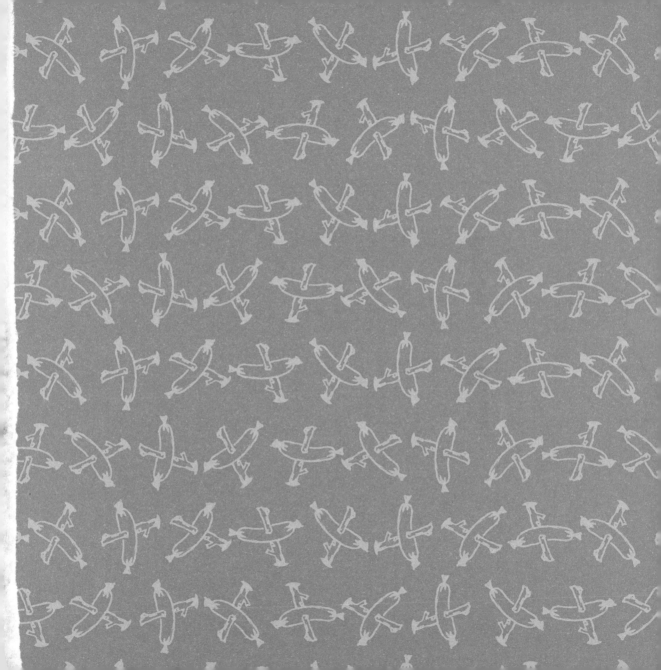

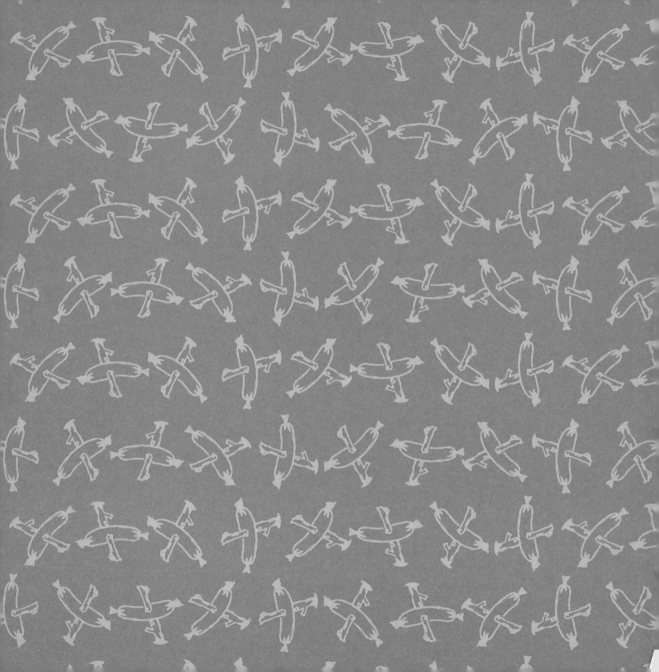